OUTRE-MER;
A PILGRIMAGE
BEYOND THE SEA.

MORE WILDSIDE CLASSICS

OUTRE-MER; A PILGRIMAGE BEYOND THE SEA.

HENRY WADSWORTH LONGFELLOW

WILDSIDE PRESS

OUTRE-MER; A PILGRIMAGE BEYOND THE SEA

This edition published in 2007 by Wildside Press, LLC.
www.wildsidebooks.com

VOLUME I.

I have passed manye landes and manye yles and contrees, and cherched manye fulle straunge places, and have ben in manye a fulle gode honourable companye. Now I am comen home to reste. And thus recordynge the tyme passed, I have fulfilled these thynges and putte hem wryten in this boke, as it woulde come into my mynde.

— Sir John Maundeville.

THE EPISTLE DEDICATORY.

The cheerful breeze sets fair; we fill our sail,
And scud before it. When the critic starts,
And angrily unties his bags of wind,
Then we lay to, and let the blast go by.

— Hurdis.

WORTHY AND
GENTLE READER!

I dedicate this little book to thee with many fears and misgivings of heart. Being a stranger to thee, and having never administered to thy wants nor to thy pleasures, I can ask nothing at thy hands, saving the common courtesies of life. Perchance, too, what I have written will be little to thy taste;—for it is little in accordance with the stirring spirit of the present age. If se, I crave thy forbearance for having thought, that even the busiest mind might not be a stranger to those moments of repose, when the clock of time clicks drowsily behind the door, and trifles become the amusement of the wise and great.

Besides, what perils await the adventurous author, who launches forth into the uncertain current of public favor in so frail a bark as this! The very rocking of the tide may overset him; or peradventure some freebooting critic, prowling about the great ocean of letters, may descry his strange colors,—hail him through a gray goose-quill, and perhaps sink him without ceremony. Indeed, the success of an unknown author is as uncertain as the wind. "When a book is first to appear in the world," says a celebrated French writer, "one knows not whom to consult to learn its destiny. The stars preside not over its nativity. Their influences have no operation on it; and the most confident astrologers dare not foretell the diverserisks of fortune it must run."

It is from such considerations, Worthy Reader, that I would fain bespeak thy friendly offices at the outset. But in asking these, I would not forestall thy good opinion too far, lest in the sequel I should disappoint thy kind wishes. I ask only a welcome and godspeed; hoping, that when thou hast read these pages, thou wilt say to me in the words of Nick Bottom, the weaver, "I shall desire you of more acquaintance, good master Cobweb."

Very sincerely thine,

THE AUTHOR.

THE PILGRIM OF OUTRE-MER.

Si j'ai long tems été en Romanie,
Et outre-mer fait mon pelerinage.
— Thibaut, Roi De Navarre.

THE PILGRIM OF OUTRE-MER.

I am a Palmer, as ye se,
Whiche of my lyfe muche part have spent,
In many a fayre and farre cuntrie,
As pilgrims do of good intent.

— The Four P's.

'Lystenyth ye godely gentylmen, and all that ben hereyn!' I am a pilgrim benighted on my way, and crave a shelter till the storm is over, and a seat by the fireside in this honorable company. As a stranger I claim this courtesy at your hands; and will repay your hospitable welcome with tales of the countries I have passed through in my pilgrimage.

This is a custom of the olden time. In the days of Chivalry and romance, every baron bold, perched aloof in his feudal castle, welcomed the stranger to his halls, and listened with delight to the pilgrim's tale, and the song of the troubadour. Both pilgrim and troubadour had their tales of wonder from a distant land, embellished with the magic of oriental exaggeration. Their salutation was,

'Lordyng lysnith to my tale,
That is meryer than the nightingale.'

The soft luxuriance of the eastern clime bloomed in the song of the bard; and the wild and romantic tales of regions so far off, as to be regarded as almost a fairy land, were well suited to the childish credulity of an age, when what is now called the old world was in its childhood. Those times have passed away. The world has grown wiser and less credulous; — and the tales, which then delighted, delight no longer. But man has not changed his nature. He still retains the same curiosity — the same love of novelty — the same fondness for romance, and tales by the chimney corner — and the same desire of wearing out the rainy day and the long winter evening with the illusions of fancy, and the fairy sketches of the poet's imagination. — It is as true now as ever, that

'Off talys, and tryfulles, many man tellys;
Sume byn trew, and sume byn ellis;
A man may dryfe forthe the day that long tyme dwellis
Wyth harpyng and pipyng, and other mery spellis,
Wyth gle, and wyth game.'

The *Pays d'Outre-Mer*, or the Land beyond the Sea, is a name by which the pilgrims and crusaders of old usually designated the Holy Land. I, too, in a certain sense, have been a pilgrim of Outre-Mer; for to my youthful imagination the old world was a kind of Holy Land, lying afar off beyond the blue horizon of the ocean; and when its shores first rose upon my sight, looming through the hazy atmosphere of the sea, my heart swelled with the deep emotions of the pilgrim, when he sees afar the spire which rises above the shrine of his devotion.

In this my pilgrimage "I have passed many lands, and countries, and searched many full strange places." I have traversed France from Normandy to Navarre; — smoked my pipe in a Flemish inn; — floated through Holland in a Trekschuit; trimmed my midnight lamp in a German university; wandered and mused amid the classic scenes of Italy; and listened to the gay guitar and merry castanet on the borders of the blue Guadalquiver. The recollection of many of the scenes I have passed through is still fresh in my mind; whilst the memory of others is fast fading away, or is blotted out forever. But now I will stay the too busy hand of time, and call back the shadowy past. Perchance the old and the wise may accuse me of frivolity; but I see in this fair company the bright eye and listening ear of youth, — an age less rigid in its censure and more willing to be pleased. "To gentlewomen and their loves is consecrated all the wooing language, allusions to love-passions, and sweet embracements feigned by the muse, mongst hills and rivers; — whatsoever tastes of description, battell, story, abstruse antiquity, and law of the kingdome, to the more severe critic. To the one, be contenting enjoyments of their auspicious desires: to the other, a happy attendance of their chosen muses."[1]

And now, fair Dames, and courteous Gentlemen, give me attentive audience; —

> *'Lordyng lystnith to my tale,*
> *That is meryer than the nightingale.'*

---

1   Selden's "Prefatory Discourse" to the notes in *Drayton's Poly-Olbion*.

THE NORMAN DILIGENCE.

Crack, crack, — crack, crack; — what a fuss thou makest? — as if it concerned the good people to be informed, that a man with a pale face and clad in black, had the honor to be driven into Paris at nine o'clock at night, by a postillion in a tawny yellow jerkin, turned up with red calamanco!

— Sterne.

THE NORMAN DILIGENCE.

The French guides, otherwise called the Postilians, have one most diabolicall custome in their travelling upon the wayes. Diabolicall it may be well called: for whensoever their horses doe a little anger them, they will say in their fury Allons diable, that is, go thou divel. This I know by mine own experience.

— Coryat's Crudities.

It was early in the "leafy month of June," that I travelled through the beautiful province of Normandy. As France was the first foreign country I visited, every thing wore an air of freshness and novelty, which pleased my eye, and kept my fancy constantly busy. Life was like a dream. It was a luxury to breathe again the free air, after having been so long cooped up at sea: and, like a long-imprisoned bird let loose from its cage, my imagination revelled in the freshness and sunshine of the morning landscape. On every side, valley and hill were covered with a carpet of soft velvet green. The birds were singing merrily in the trees, and the landscape wore that look of gaiety so well described in the quaint language of an old romance, making the "sad, pensive, and aching heart to rejoice, and to throw off mourning and sadness." Here and there a cluster of chestnut trees shaded a thatch-roofed cottage, and little patches of vineyard were scattered on the slope of the hills, mingling their delicate green with the deep hues of the early summer grain. The whole landscape had a fresh, breezy look. It was not hedged in from the highways, but lay open to the eye of the traveller, and seemed to welcome him with open arms. I felt less a stranger in the land: and as my eye traced the dusty road winding along through a rich cultivated country, and skirted on either side with blossomed fruit trees, and occasionally caught glimpses of a little farm-house resting in a green hollow, and lapped in the bosom of plenty, I felt that I was in a prosperous, hospitable, and happy land.

I had taken my seat on top of the Diligence, in order to have a better view of the country. It was one of those ponderous vehicles, which totter slowly along the paved roads of France, laboring beneath a mountain of trunks and bales of all descriptions, and, like the Trojan horse, bore a groaning multitude within it. It was a curious and cumbersome machine, resembling the bodies of three coaches placed upon one carriage, with a cabriolet on top for outside passengers. On the pannels of each door were painted the fleurs-de-lis of France, and upon the side of the coach emblazoned in golden characters: *"Exploitation Générale des Messageries Royales des Diligences pour le Havre, Rouen et Paris."*

It would be useless to describe the motley groups, that filled the four quarters of this little world. There was the dusty tradesman, with green coat and cotton umbrella; the sallow invalid, in skull-cap, and cloth shoes; the priest in his cassock; the peasant in his frock; and a whole family of squalling children. My fellow travellers on top were a gay subaltern, with fierce mustaches, and a nut-brown village beauty of sweet sixteen.

The subaltern wore a military undress, and a little blue cloth cap in the shape of a cow-bell, trimmed smartly with silver lace, and cocked on one side of his head. The brunette was decked out with a staid white Norman cap, nicely starched and plaited, and nearly three feet high; a rosary and cross about her neck; a linsey-woolsey gown, and wooden shoes.

The personage who seemed to rule this little world with absolute sway, was a short pursy man, with a busy, self-satisfied air, and the sonorous title of *Monsieur le Conducteur.* As insignia of office, he wore a little round fur cap, and fur-trimmed jacket; and carried in his hand a small leathern port folio, containing his way-bill. He sat with us on top of the Diligence, and with comic gravity issued his mandates to the postillion below, like some petty monarch speaking from his throne. In every dingy village we thundered through, he had a thousand commissions to execute and to receive: a package to throw out on this side, and another to take in on that: a whisper for the landlady at the inn: a love-letter and a kiss for her daughter: and a wink, or a snap of his fingers for the chamber-maid at the window. Then there were so many questions to be asked and answered, while changing horses! Every body had a word to say. It was Monsieur le Conducteur! here; Monsieur le Conducteur! there. He was in complete bustle; till at length crying *en route!* he ascended the dizzy height and we lumbered away in a cloud of dust.

But what most attracted my attention was the grotesque appearance of the postillion and the horses. He was a comical looking little fellow, already past the heyday of life, with a thin, sharp countenance, to which the smoke of tobacco and the fumes of wine had given the dusty look of wrinkled parchment. He was equipped in a short jacket of purple velvet, set off with a red collar, and adorned with silken cord. Tight pantaloons of bright yellow leather arrayed his pipe-stem legs, which were swallowed up in a huge pair of wooden boots, iron-fastened, and armed with long, rattling spurs. His shirt-collar was of vast dimensions, and between it and the broad brim of his high, bell-crowned, varnished hat, projected an eel-skin queue, with a little tuft of frizzled hair, like a powder-puff at the end, bobbing up and down with the motion of the rider, and scattering a white cloud around him.

The horses, which drew the Diligence, were harnessed to it with ropes and leather, and in the most uncouth manner imaginable. They were five in number: — black, white, and gray; as various in size as in color. Their tails were braided and tied up with wisps of straw; and when the postillion mounted and cracked his heavy whip, off they started, one pulling this way, another that; one on the gallop, another trotting and the rest dragging along at a scrambling pace, between a trot and a walk. No sooner did the vehicle get comfortably in motion, than the postillion, throwing the reins upon his horse's neck, and drawing a flint and steel from one pocket, and a short-stemmed pipe from another, leisurely struck fire, and began to smoke. Ever and anon some part of the rope harness would give way; Monsieur le Conducteur from on high would thunder forth an oath or two; a head would be popped out at every window: half a dozen voices exclaim at once, "what's the matter?" and the postillion, apostrophizing the diable as usual, thrust his long whip into the leg of his boot, leisurely dismount, and drawing a handful of packthread from his pocket, quietly set himself to mend matters in the best way possible.

In this manner we toiled slowly along the dusty highway. Occasionally the scene was enlivened by a group of peasants, driving before them a little ass, laden with vegetables for a neighboring market. Then we would pass a solitary shepherd, sitting by the road-side, with a shaggy dog at his feet, guarding his flock, and making his scanty meal on the contents of his wallet; or perchance a little peasant girl, in wooden shoes, leading a cow, by a cord attached to her horns, to browse along the side of the ditch. Then we would all alight to ascend some formidable hill on foot, and be escorted up by a clamorous troop of sturdy mendicants, — annoyed by the ceaseless importunity of worthless beggary, or moved to pity by the palsied limbs of the aged, and the sightless eyeballs of the blind.

Occasionally, too, the postillion drew up in front of a dingy little cabaret, completely overshadowed by wide-spreading trees. A lusty grape-vine clambered up beside the door; and a pine bough was thrust out from a hole in the wall, by way of tavern bush. Upon the front of the house was generally inscribed in large black letters; "ICI ON DONNE A BOIRE ET A MANGER; ON LOGE

A PIED ET A CHEVAL;" a sign which may be thus paraphrased; "Good Entertainment for man and beast;" but which was once translated by a foreigner, "Here they give to eat and drink; they lodge on foot and on horse-back!"

Thus one object of curiosity succeeded another; hill, valley, stream and woodland flitted by me like the shifting scenes of a magic lantern, and one train of thought gave place to another; till at length in the after part of the day, we entered the broad and shady avenue of fine old trees, which leads to the western gate of Rouen, and a few moments afterwards, were lost in the crowds and confusion of its narrow streets.

THE GOLDEN LION INN, AT ROUEN.

He is a traveller into former times, whence he hath learnt their language and fashions. If he meets with an old manuscript, which hath the mark worn out of its mouth, and hath lost the date, yet he can tell the age thereof, either by the phrase or character.

— Fuller's *True Church Antiquary.*

THE GOLDEN LION INN.

*Monsieur Vinot. Je veux absolument un Lion d'Or;
parce qu'on dit, Où allez-vous? Au Lion d'Or! — D'où
venez-vous? Du Lion d'Or! — Où irons-nous? Au Lion
d'Or! — Où y a-t-il de bon vin? Au Lion d'Or!*
                                        — La Rose Rouge.

This answer of Monsieur Vinot must have been running in
my head, as the Diligence stopped at the Messagerie; for when the
porter, who took my luggage, said;

"Où allez-vous, Monsieur?"

I answered, without thinking, (for be it said with all the
veracity of a traveller, at that time I did not know there was a
Golden Lion in the city)

"Au Lion d'Or."

And so to the Lion d'Or we went.

The hostess of the Golden Lion received me with a courtesy
and a smile, rang the house-bell for a servant — and told him to
take the gentleman's things to No. 35. I followed him up stairs.
One — two — three — four — five — six — seven! Seven stories
high — by our Lady! — I counted them every one; — and when I
went down to remonstrate, I counted them again; so that there
was no possibility of a mistake. When I asked for a lower room,
the hostess told me the house was full; and when I spake of going
to another hotel, she said she should be so very sorry, so désolée,
to have Monsieur leave her, that I marched up again to No. 35.

After finding all the fault I could with the chamber, I ended, as
is generally the case with most men on such occasions, by being
very well pleased with it. The only thing I could possibly complain
of, was my being lodged in the seventh story, and in the immediate neighborhood of a gentleman who was learning to play the
French horn. But to remunerate me for these disadvantages, my
window looked down into a market-place, and gave me a distant
view of the towers of the Cathedral, and the ruins of the church
and Abbey of Saint-Ouen.

When I had fully prepared myself for a ramble through the
city, it was already sundown; and after the heat and dust of the
day, the freshness of the long evening twilight was delightful.
When I enter a new city, I cannot rest till I have satisfied the first
cravings of curiosity by rambling through its streets. Nor can I
endure a Cicerone, with his eternal "This way, Sir." I never desire
to be led directly to an object worthy of a traveller's notice, but

prefer a thousand times, to find my own way, and come upon it by surprise. This was particularly the case at Rouen. It was the first European city of importance that I visited. There was an air of antiquity about the whole city, that breathed of the Middle Ages; and so strong and delightful was the impression, that it made upon my youthful imagination, that nothing, which I afterwards saw, could either equal or efface it. I have since passed through that city; but I did not stop. I was unwilling to destroy an impression, which, even at this distant day, is as fresh upon my mind, as if it were of yesterday.

With these delightful feelings I rembled on from street to street, till at length after threading a narrow alley, I unexpectedly came out in front of the magnificent Cathedral. If it had suddenly risen from the earth, the effect could not have been more powerful and instantaneous. It completely overwhelmed my imagination; and I stood for a long time motionless, and gazing entranced upon the stupendous edifice. I had seen no specimen of gothic architecture before, save the remains of a little church at Havre; and the massive towers before me — the lofty windows of stained glass — the low portal, with its receding arches and rude statues — all produced upon my untravelled mind an impression of awful sublimity. When I entered the church, the impression was still more deep and solemn. It was the hour of vespers. The religious twilight of the place — the lamps that burned on the distant altar — the kneeling crowd — the tinkling bell — and the chaunt of the evening service, that rolled along the vaulted roof in broken and repeated echoes — filled me with new and intense emotions. When I gazed on the stupendous architecture of the church — the huge columns, that the eye followed up till they were lost in the gathering dusk of the arches above — the long and shadowy aisles — the statues of saints and martyrs, that stood in every recess — the figures of armed knights upon the tombs — the uncertain light, that stole through the painted windows of each little chapel — and the form of the cowled and solitary monk, kneeling at the shrine of his favorite saint, or passing between the lofty columns of the church, — all I had read of, but had not seen, — I was transported back to the Dark Ages, and felt as I shall never feel again.

On the following day I visited the remains of an old palace, built by Edward the Third, now occupied as the Palais de Justice; and the ruins of the church and monastery of Saint Antoine. — I saw the hole in the tower where the ponderous bell of the Abbey fell through; — and took a peep at the curious illuminated manuscript of Daniel d'Aubonne in the public library. The remainder of the morning was spent in visiting the ruins of the ancient Abbey of St. Ouen, which is now transformed into the Hotel de Ville, and in strolling through its beautiful gardens, dreaming of the present and the past, and given up to "a melancholy of my own."

At the *Table d' Hôte* of the Golden Lion, I fell into conversation with an elderly gentleman, who proved to be a great antiquarian, and thoroughly read in all the forgotten lore of the city. As our tastes were somewhat similar, we were soon upon very friendly terms; and after dinner, we strolled out to visit some remarkable localities, and took the gloriatogether in the Chevalier Bayard.

When we returned to the Golden Lion he entertained me with many curious stories of the spots we had been visiting. Among others he related the following singular adventure of a monk of the Abbey of Saint Antoine, which amused me so much, that I cannot refrain from presenting it to my readers. I will not, however, vouch for the truth of the story; for that the antiquarian himself would not do. He said he found it in an ancient manuscript of the Middle Ages, in the archives of the public library, and I give it as it was told me, without note or comment.

MARTIN FRANC AND THE MONK OF SAINT ANTHONY.

Seignor, oiez une merveille,
C'onques n'oïstes sa pareille,
Que je vos vueil dire et conter;
Or metez cuer a l'escouter.
— Fabliau du Bouchier d'Abbeville.

Lystyn Lordyngs to my tale,
And ye shall here of one story,
Is better than any wyne or ale,
That ever was made in this cuntry.
— Ancient Metrical Romance.

MARTIN FRANC AND THE
MONK OF SAINT ANTHONY.

Quoth hee, heer is a chaunce for the nones,
For heer hangeth the false Munk by cocks bones.
— The Mery Jest of Dane Hew.

In times of old there lived in the city of Rouen a tradesman, named Martin Franc, who, by a series of misfortunes, had been reduced from oppulence to poverty. But poverty, which generally makes men humble and laborious, only served to make him proud and lazy: and in proportion as he grew poorer and poorer, he grew also prouder and lazier. He contrived, however, to live along from day to day, by now and then pawning a silken robe of his wife, or selling a silver spoon, or some other trifle saved from the wreck of his better fortune; and passed his time pleasantly enough in loitering about the market place, and walking up and down on the sunny side of the street.

The fair Marguerite, his wife, was celebrated through the whole city for her beauty, her wit, and her virtue. She was a brunette, with the blackest eye — the whitest teeth — and the ripest nut-brown cheek in all Normandy; — her figure was tall and stately — her hands and feet most delicately moulded — and her swimming gait like the motion of a swan. In happier days she had been the delight of the richest tradesmen in the city, and the envy of the fairest dames; and when she became poor, her fame was not a little increased by her cruelty to several substantial burghers, who, without consulting their wives, had generously offered to stand between her husband and bankruptcy, and do all in their power to raise a worthy and respectable family.

The friends of Martin Franc, like the friends of many a ruined man before and since, deserted him in the day of adversity. Of all that had eaten his dinners, and drunk his wine, and philandered with his wife, none sought the narrow alley and humble dwelling of the broken tradesman, save one; and that one was Friar Gui, the sacristan of the Abbey of Saint Anthony. He was a little, jolly, red-faced friar, with a leer in his eye, and rather a naughty reputation for a man of his cloth; but as he was a kind of travelling gazette and always brought the latest news and gossip of the city, and besides was the only person that condescended to visit the house of Martin Franc, — in fine, for the want of a better, he was considered in the light of a friend.

In these constant assiduities, Friar Gui had his secret motives, of which the single heart of Martin Franc was entirely unsuspicious. The keener eye of his wife, however, soon discovered two faces under the hood. She observed that the Friar generally timed his visits so as to be at the house when Martin Franc was not at home, — that he seemed to prefer the edge of the evening, — and that as his visits became more frequent he always had some little apology ready, such as 'being obliged to pass that way, he could not go by the door without just dropping in to see how the good man Martin did.' — Occasionally, too, he ventured to bring her some ghostly present — such as a picture of the Madonna and child, or one of those little naked images, which are hawked about the streets at the Nativity. Though the object of all this was but too obvious, yet the fair Marguerite perserved in misconstruing the Friar's intentions, and in dexterously turning aside any expressions of gallantry that fell from his venerable lips. In this way Friar Gui was for a long time kept at bay; and Martin Franc preserved in the day of poverty and distress, that consolation of all this world's afflictions — a friend. But finally things came to such a pass that the honest tradesman opened his eyes, and wondered he had been asleep so long. Whereupon he was irreverend enough to tweak the nose of Friar Gui, and then to thrust him into the street by the shoulders.

Meanwhile the times grew worse and worse. One family relic followed another; — the last silken robe was pawned: — the last silver spoon sold; until at length poor Martin Franc was forced to 'drag the devil by the tail;' — in other words, beggary stared him full in the face. But the fair Marguerite did not even then despair. In those days a belief in the immediate guardianship of the saints, was much more strong and prevalent than in these lewd and degenerate times; and as there seemed no great probability of improving their condition by any lucky change, which could be brought about by mere human agency, she determined to try what could be done by intercession with the patron saint of her husband. Accordingly she repaired one evening to the Abbey of Saint Anthony, to place a votive candle and offer her prayer at the altar, which stood in the little chapel dedicated to Saint Martin.

It was already sun-down when she reached the church, and the evening service of the Virgin had commenced. A cloud of incense floated before the altar of the Madonna, and the organ rolled its deep melody along the dim arches of the church. Marguerite mingled with the kneeling crowd, and repeated the responses in Latin, with as much devotion, as the most learned clerk of the convent. When the service was over, she repaired to the chapel of Saint Martin, and lighting her votive tapes at the silver lamp, which burned before his altar, knelt down in a retired part of the chapel, and, with tears in her eyes, besought the saint for aid and protection. Whilst she was thus engaged, the church became gradually deserted, till she was left, as she thought, alone. But in this she was mistaken; for when she arose to depart, the portly figure of Friar Gui was standing close at her elbow!

"A fair, good evening to my lady Marguerite," said he significantly. "Saint Martin has heard your prayer, and sent me to relieve your poverty."

"Then, by the Virgin!" replied she, "the good saint is not very fastidious in the choice of his messengers."

"Nay, good wife;" answered the Friar, not at all abashed by this ungracious reply; "if the tidings are good, what matters it who the messenger may be? — And how does Martin Franc, these days?"

"He is well, Sir Gui;" replied Marguerite; "and were he present, I doubt not would thank you heartily for the interest you still take in him and his poor wife."

"He has done me wrong;" continued the Friar, without seeming to notice the pointedness of Marguerite's reply. "But it is our duty to forgive our enemies; and so let the past be forgotten. I know that he is in want. Here, take this to him, and tell him I am still his friend."

So saying, he drew a small purse from the sleeve of his habit, and proffered it to his companion. — I know not whether it were a suggestion of Saint Martin, but true it is, that the fair lady of Martin Franc seemed to lend a more willing ear to the earnest whispers of the Friar. At length she said;

"Put up your purse; to-day I can neither deliver your gift nor your message. Martin Franc has gone from home."

"Then keep it for yourself."

"Nay, Sir Monk;" replied Marguerite, casting down her eyes; "I can take no bribes here in the church, and in the very chapel of my husband's patron saint. You shall bring it to me at my house, an' you will, Sir Gui."

The Friar put up the purse, and the conversation, which followed, was in a low and indistinct undertone, audible only to the ears for which it was intended. At length the interview ceased; and, — O Woman! the last words that the virtuous Marguerite uttered, as she glided from the church, were;

"To-night; — when the Abbey clock strikes twelve! —

remember!"

It would be useless to relate how impatiently the Friar counted the hours and the quarters, as they chimed from the ancient tower of the Abbey, whilst he paced to and fro along the gloomy cloister. At length the appointed hour approached; and just before the convent bell sent forth its summons to call the friars of Saint Anthony to their midnight devotions, a figure, with a cowl, stole out of a postern gate and passing silently along the deserted streets, soon turned into the little alley, which led to the dwelling of Martin Franc. It was none other than Friar Gui. He rapped softly at the tradesman's door; and casting a look up and down the street, as if to assure himself that his motions were unobserved, slipped into the house.

"Has Martin Franc returned?" enquired he in a whisper.

"No;" answered the sweet voice of his wife; "he will not be back to night."

"Then all good angels befriend us!" continued the monk, endeavoring to take her hand.

"Not so, Sir Monk," said she, disengaging herself. You forget the conditions of our meeting."

The Friar paused a moment; and then drawing a heavy leathern purse from his girdle, he threw it upon the table. At the same moment a footstep was heard behind him, and a heavy blow from a club threw him prostrate upon the floor. It came from the strong arm of Martin Franc himself!

It is hardly necessary to say that his absence was feigned. His wife had invented the story to decoy the lecherous monk, and thereby to keep her husband from beggary and to relieve herself, once for all, from the importunities of a false friend. At first Martin Franc would not listen to the proposition; but at length he yielded to the urgent entreaties of his wife; and the plan finally agreed upon was, that Friar Gui, after leaving his purse behind him, should be sent back to the convent with a severer discipline than his shoulders had ever received from any penitence of his own.

The affair, however, took a more serious turn than was intended; for when they tried to raise the Friar from the ground, — he was dead. The blow aimed at his shoulders fell upon his shaven crown; and in the excitement of the moment Martin Franc had dealt a heavier stroke than he intended. Amid the grief and consternation, which followed this discovery, the quick imagination of his wife suggested an expedient of safety. A bunch of keys at the Friar's girdle caught her eye. Hastily unfastening the ring, she gave the keys to her husband, exclaiming;

"For the holy Virgin's sake, be quick! One of these keys unlocks the postern gate of the convent garden. Carry the body thither, and leave it among the trees!"

Martin Franc threw the dead body of the monk across his shoulders, and with a heavy heart took the way to the abbey. It was a clear starry night; and though the moon had not yet risen, her light was in the sky, and came reflected down in a soft twilight upon earth. Not a sound was heard through all the long and solitary streets, save at intervals the distant crowing of a cock, or the melancholy hoot of an owl from the lofty tower of the abbey. The silence weighed like an accusing spirit upon the guilty conscience of Martin Franc. He started at the sound of his own breathing, as he panted under the heavy burden of the monk's body; and if perchance a bat flitted near him on drowsy wings, he paused, and his heart beat audibly with terror: such cowards does conscience make of even the most courageous. At length he reached the garden wall of the abbey, — opened the postern gate with the key, and bearing the monk into the garden, seated him upon a stone bench by the edge of the fountain, with his head resting against a column, upon which was sculptured an image of the Madonna. He then replaced the bunch of keys at the monk's girdle, and returned home with hasty steps.

When the Prior of the convent, to whom the repeated delinquencies of Friar Gui were but too well known, observed that he was again absent from his post at midnight prayers, he waxed exceedingly angry; and no sooner were the duties of the chapel finished, than he sent a monk in pursuit of the truant sacristan, summoning him to appear immediately at his cell. By chance it happened, that the monk, chosen for this duty, was a bitter enemy of Friar Gui; and very shrewdly supposing that the sacristan had stolen out of the garden gate on some midnight adventure, he took that direction in pursuit. The moon was just climbing the convent wall, and threw its silvery light through the trees of the garden, and on the sparkling waters of the fountain, that fell with a soft lulling sound into the deep basin below. As the monk passed on his way, he stopped to quench his thirst with a draught of the cool water, and was turning to depart when his eye caught the motionless form of the sacristan, sitting erect in the shadow of the stone column.

"How is this, Friar Gui?" quoth the monk. "Is this a place to be sleeping at midnight, when the brotherhood are all in their dormitories?" Friar Gui made no answer.

"Up, up! — thou eternal sleeper, and do penance for thy negligence. The prior calls for thee at his cell!" continued the monk, growing angry, and shaking the sacristan by the shoulder.

But still no answer.

"Then by Saint Anthony I'll wake thee! So, so! Sir Gui!" —

And saying this he dealt the sacristan a heavy box on the ear. The body bent slowly forward from its erect position, and giving a headlong plunge, sank with a heavy splash into the basin of the fountain. The monk waited a few moments in expectation of seeing Friar Gui rise dripping from his cold bath, but he waited in vain; — for he lay motionless at the bottom of the basin — his eyes open, and his ghastly face distorted by the ripples of the water. With a beating heart the monk stooped down and grasping the skirt of the sacristan's habit, at length succeeded in drawing him from the water. All efforts, however, to resuscitate him were unavailing. The monk was filled with terror, not doubting that the Friar had died untimely by his hand; and as the animosity between them was no secret in the convent, he feared that, when the deed was known, he should be accused of wilful murder. He therefore looked round for an expedient to relieve himself of the dead body; and the well-known character of the sacristan soon suggested one. He determined to carry the body to the house of the most noted beauty of Rouen, and leave it on the door stop so that all suspicion of the murder might fall upon the shoulders of some jealous husband. The beauty of Martin Franc's wife had penetrated even the thick walls of the convent, and there was not a friar in the whole Abbey of Saint Anthony who had not done penance for his truant imagination. — Accordingly the dead body of Friar Gui was laid upon the monk's brawny shoulders, — carried back to the house of Martin Franc, and placed in an erect position against the door. The monk knocked loud and long; and then gliding through a bylane, stole back to the convent.

A troubled conscience would not suffer Martin Franc and his wife to close their eyes; but they lay awake lamenting the doleful events of the night. The knock at the door sounded like a death-knell in their ears. It still continued at intervals, rap — rap — rap! — with a dull, low sound, — as if something heavy were swinging against the pannel; for the wind had risen during the night and every angry gust that swept down the alley, swung the arms of the lifeless sacristan against the door. At length Martin Franc mustered courage enough to dress himself and to go down, whilst his wife followed him with a lamp in her hand; but no sooner had he lifted the latch, than the ponderous body of Friar

Gui fell stark and heavy into his arms.

"Jesu Maria!" exclaimed Marguerite, crossing herself; — "here is the monk again!"

"Yes, and dripping wet, as if he had just been dragged out of the river!"

"O we are betrayed — betrayed!" exclaimed Marguerite in agony.

"Then the devil himself has betrayed us;" replied Martin Franc, disengaging himself from the embrace of the sacristan; "for I met not a living being; the whole city was as silent as the grave." "Holy Saint Martin defend us!" continued his terrified wife. "Here, take this scapulary to guard you from the evil one; — and lose no time. You must throw the body into the river; or we are lost! Holy Virgin! How bright the moon shines!"

Saying this she threw round his neck a scapulary — with the figure of a cross on one end and an image of the Virgin on the other, and Martin Franc again took the dead Friar upon his shoulders and with fearful misgivings departed on his dismal errand. He kept as much as possible in the shadow of the houses, and had nearly reached the quay, when suddenly, he thought he heard footsteps behind him. — He stopped to listen; it was no mistake — they came along the pavement, tramp! — tramp! and every step grew louder and nearer. Martin Franc tried to quicken his pace; — but in vain; — his knees smote together, and he staggered against the wall. His hand relaxed its grasp; and the monk slid from his back, and stood ghastly and straight beside him, supported by chance against the shoulder of his bearer. At that moment, a man came round the corner, tottering beneath the weight of a huge sack. As his head was bent downwards, he did not perceive Martin Franc, till he was close upon him; and when, on looking up, he saw two figures standing motionless in the shadow of the wall, he thought himself waylaid, and, without waiting to be assaulted, dropped the sack from his shoulders, and ran off at full speed. The sack fell heavily on the pavement, and directly at the feet of Martin Franc. In the fall the string was broken; and out came the bloody head — not of a dead monk, as it first seemed to the excited imagination of Martin Franc, — but of a dead hog! — When the terror and surprise caused by this singular event had a little subsided, an idea came into the mind of Martin Franc, very similar to what would have come into the mind of almost any person in similar circumstances. He took the hog out of the sack and putting the body of the monk into its place, secured it well with the remnants of the broken string; and then hurried homeward with the hog upon his shoulders.

He was hardly out of sight, when the man of the sack returned, accompanied by two others. They were surprised to find the sack still lying on the ground, with no one near it, and began to jeer the former bearer, telling him he had been frightened at his own shadow on the wall. Then one of them took the sack upon his shoulders, without the least suspicion of the change that had been made in its contents, and all three disappeared.

Now it happened that the city of Rouen was at that time infested by three street robbers, who walked in darkness like the pestilence, and always carried the plunder of their midnight marauding to the *Tête-de-Bœuf*, a little tavern in one of the darkest and narrowest lanes of the city. The host of the *Tête-de-Bœuf* was privy to all their schemes, and had an equal share in the profits of their nightly excursions. He gave a helping hand, too, by the length of his bills, and by plundering the pockets of any chance traveller, that was luckless enough to sleep under his roof.

On the night of the disastrous adventure of Friar Gui, this little marauding party had been prowling about the city until a late hour, without finding any thing to reward their labors. At length, however, they chanced to spy a hog, hanging under a shed in a butcher's yard in readiness for the next day's market; and as they were not very fastidious in selecting their plunder, but on the contrary rather addicted to taking whatever they could lay their hands on, the hog was straightway purloined, thrust into a large sack, and sent to the *Tête-de-Bœuf* on the shoulders of one of the party, whilst the other two continued their nocturnal excursion. It was this person, who had been so terrified at the appearance of Martin Franc and the dead monk; and as this encounter had interrupted any further operations of the party — the dawn of day being now near at hand, — they all repaired to their gloomy den in the *Tête-de-Bœuf*. The host was impatiently waiting their return; and, asking what plunder they had brought with them, proceeded without delay to remove it from the sack. The first thing that presented itself, on untying the string, was the monk's hood.

"The devil take the devil!" cried host, as he opened the neck of the sack, "What's this? — Your hog has got a cowl!"

"The poor devil has become disgusted with the world, and turned monk!" said he, who held the light, a little surprised at seeing the head covered with a coarse gray cloth.

"Sure enough he has," exclaimed another, starting back in dismay, as the shaven crown and ghastly face of the Friar appeared. "Holy Saint Benedict be with us! — It is a monk, stark dead!"

"A dead monk, indeed!" said a third, with an incredulous shake of the head, "How could a dead monk get into this sack?" — No, no: there is some diablerie in this. I have heard it said, that Satan can take any shape he pleases; and you may rely upon it, this is Satan himself, who has taken the shape of a monk to get us all hanged."

"Then we had better kill the devil than have the devil kill us!" — replied the host, crossing himself. "And the sooner we do it, the better; for it is now near day-light, and people will soon be passing in the street."

"So say I;" rejoined the man of magic; "and my advice is to take him to the butcher's yard, and hang him up in the place where we found the hog."

This proposition so pleased the others, that it was executed without delay. They carried the Friar to the butcher's house, and passing a strong cord round his neck, suspended him to a beam in the shed, and there left him.

When the night was at length passed, and daylight began to peep into the eastern windows of the city, the butcher arose, and prepared himself for market. He was casting up in his mind, what the hog would bring at his stall, when looking upward — lo! in its place he recognized the dead body of Friar Gui.

"By Saint Dennis!" quoth the butcher, "I always feared that this Friar would not die quietly in his cell; but I never thought I should find him hanging under my own roof. — This must not be; it will be said, that I murdered him, and I shall pay for it with my life. I must contrive some way to get rid of him."

So saying he called his man, and showing him what had been done, asked him how he should dispose of the body, so that he might not be accused of murder. The man, who was of a ready wit, reflected a moment, and then answered;

"This is indeed a difficult matter; but there is no evil without its remedy. — We will place the friar on horseback —"

"What! — a dead man on horseback? — impossible!" interrupted the butcher. "Who ever heard of a dead man on horseback!"

"Hear me out, and then judge. We must place the body on horseback, as well as we may, and bind it fast with cords, and then set the horse loose in the street, and pursue after him crying out, that the monk has stolen the horse. Thus all who meet him will strike him with their staves, as he passes, and it will be thought that he came to his death in that way."

Though this seemed to the butcher rather a mad project, yet, as no better one offered itself, at the moment, and there was no time for reflection, mad as the project was, they determined to put it into execution. Accordingly the butcher's horse was brought out, and the Friar was bound upon his back, and with much difficulty fixed in an upright position. The butcher then gave the horse a blow upon the crupper with his staff, which set him into a smart gallop down the street, and he and his man joined in pursuit crying;

"Stop thief! — Stop thief! — The friar has stolen my horse!"

As it was now sunrise the streets were full of people, peasants driving their goods to market, and citizens going to their daily avocations. When they saw the Friar dashing at full speed down the street, they joined in the cry of "Stop thief! — Stop that horse!" and many, who endeavored to seize the bridle as the Friar passed them at full speed, were thrown upon the pavement, and trampled under foot. Others joined in the halloo! and the pursuit; but this only served to quicken the gallop of the frightened steed, who dashed down one street and up another like the wind, with two or three mounted citizens clattering in full cry at his heels. At length they reached the market place. — The people scattered right and left in dismay — and the steed and rider dashed onward, overthrowing in their course men and women, and stalls, and piles of merchandise, and sweeping away like a whirlwind. Tramp — tramp — tramp! they clattered on; they had distanced all pursuit. They reached the quay; the wide pavement was cleared at a bound — one more wild leap — and splash! — both horse and rider sank into the rapid current of the river — swept down the stream — and were seen no more!

THE VILLAGE OF AUTEUIL.

Il n'est tel plaisir
Que d'estre à gésir
Parmy les beaux champs,
L'herbe verd choisir,
Et prendre bon temps.

— Martial d'Auvergne.

THE VILLAGE OF AUTEUIL.

Oyez-vous
Ce bruit tant doux
Décliquer de la gorgette
Du geai mignot,
Du linot
Et de la frisque allouette?
                    — Bonaventure Desperriers.

The sultry heat of summer always brings with it, to the idler and the man of leisure, a longing for the leafy shade and the green luxuriance of the country. It is pleasant to interchange the din of the city, — the movement of the crowd, — and the gossip of society, with the silence of the hamlet, — the quiet seclusion of the grove, and the gossip of a woodland brook. As is sung in the old ballad of Robin Hood,

In somer when the shawes be sheyn,
And leves be large and long,
Hit is full mery in feyre foreste,
To here the foulys song.
To se the dere draw to the dale
And leve the hilles hee,
And shadow hem in the leves grene,
Vnder the grene wode tre.

It was a feeling of this kind, that prompted me during my residence in the north of France to pass one of the summer months at Auteuil — the pleasantest of the many little villages that lie in the immediate vicinity of the metropolis. It is situated on the outskirts of the Bois de Boulogne — a wood of some extent, in whose green alleys the dusty cit enjoys the luxury of an evening drive, and gentlemen meet in the morning to give each other satisfaction in the usual way. A cross road, skirted with green hedge-rows, and overshadowed by tall poplars, leads you from the noisy highway of St. Cloud and Versailles to the still retirement of this suburban hamlet. On either side, the eye discovers old chateaux amid the trees, and green parks, whose pleasant shades recall a thousand images of La Fontaine, Racine, and Molière; and on an eminence overlooking the windings of the Seine, and giving a beautiful though distant view of the domes and gardens of Paris, rises the village of Passy, long the residence of our countrymen Franklin and Count

Rumford.

I took up my abode at a *Maison de Santé*; not that I was a vale-tudinarian, — but because I there found some one to whom I could whisper, 'How sweet is solitude!' Behind the house was a garden filled with fruit trees of various kinds, and adorned with gravel walks, and green arbors, furnished with tables and rustic seats, for the repose of the invalid and the sleep of the indolent. Here the inmates of the rural hospital met on common ground, to breathe the invigorating air of morning, and while away the lazy noon or vacant evening with tales of the sick chamber.

The establishment was kept by Dr. Dent-de-lion, a dried up little fellow, with red hair, a sandy complexion, and the physiognomy and gestures of a monkey. His character corresponded to his outward lineaments; for he had all a monkey's busy and curious impertinence. Nevertheless, such as he was, the village Æsculapius strutted forth the little great man of Auteuil. The peasants looked up to him as to an oracle, — he contrived to be at the head of every thing, and laid claim to the credit of all public improvements in the village: — in fine he was a great man on a small scale.

It was within the dingy walls of this little potentate's imperial palace, that I chose my country residence. I had a chamber in the second story, with a solitary window, which looked upon the street, and gave me a peep into a neighbor's garden. This I esteemed a great privilege; for, as a stranger, I desired to see all that was passing out of doors, and the sight of green trees, though growing on another man's ground, is always a blessing. Within doors, — had I been disposed to quarrel with my household gods, — I might have taken some objection to my neighborhood; for on one side of me was a consumptive patient, whose graveyard cough drove me from my chamber by day, — and on the other, an English Colonel, whose incoherent ravings, in the delirium of a high and obstinate fever, often broke my slumbers by night. But I found ample amends for these inconveniences in the society of those, who were so little indisposed as hardly to know what ailed them, and those, who in health themselves, had accompanied a friend or relative to the shades of the country in pursuit of it. To these I am indebted for much courtesy; and particularly to one, who, if these pages should ever meet her eye, will not, I hope, be unwilling to accept this slight memorial of a former friendship.

It was, however, to the *Bois de Boulogne*, that I looked for my principal recreation. There I took my solitary walk, morning and evening; or, mounted on a little mouse-colored donkey, paced demurely along the woodland pathway. I had a favorite seat beneath the shadow of a venerable oak, one of the few hoary patriarchs of the wood, which had survived the bivouacs of the Allied Armies. It stood upon the brink of a little glassy pool, whose tranquil bosom was the image of a quiet and secluded life, and stretched its parental arms over a rustic bench, that had been constructed beneath it, for the accommodation of the foot-traveller, or, perchance, some idle dreamer like myself. It seemed to look round with a lordly air upon its old hereditary domain, whose stillness was no longer broken by the tap of the martial drum, nor the discordant clang of arms; and, as the breeze whispered among its branches, it seemed to be holding friendly colloquies with a few of its venerable cotemporaries, who stooped from the opposite bank of the pool, nodding gravely now and then, and ogling themselves with a sigh in the mirror below.

In this quiet haunt of rural repose, I used to sit at noon, — hear the birds sing, and "possess myself in much quietness." Just at my feet lay the little silver pool, with the sky and the woods painted in its mimic vault, and occasionally the image of a bird, or the soft watery outline of a cloud, floating silently through its sunny hollows. The water-lily spread its broad green leaves on the surface, and rocked to sleep a little world of insect life in its golden cradle. Sometimes a wandering leaf came floating and wavering downward, and settled on the water; then a vagabond insect would break the smooth surface into a thousand ripples, or a green-coated frog slide from the bank, and plump! — dive headlong to the bottom.

I entered, too, with some enthusiasm into all the rural sports and merrimakes of the village. The holidays were so many little eras of mirth and good feeling; for the French have that happy and sunshine temperament — that merry-go-mad character, — which makes all their social meetings scenes of enjoyment and hilarity. I made it a point never to miss any of the Fêtes Champêtres, or rural dances, at the wood of Boulogne; though I confess it sometimes gave me a momentary uneasiness to see my rustic throne beneath the oak usurped by a noisy group of girls, the silence and decorum of my imaginary realm broken by music and laughter, and, in a word, my whole kingdom turned topsyturvy, with romping, fiddling, and dancing. But I am naturally, and from principle too, a lover of all those innocent amusements, which cheer the laborer's toil, and, as it were, put their shoulders to the wheel of life, and help the poor man along with his load of cares. Hence I saw with no small delight the rustic swain astride the wooden horse of the carrousel, and the village maiden whirling round and round in its dizzy car; or took my stand on a rising ground that overlooked the dance, an idle spectator in a busy throng. It was just where the village touched the outward border of the wood. There a little area had been levelled beneath the trees, surrounded by a painted rail, with a row of benches inside. The music was placed in a slight balcony, built around the trunk of a large tree in the centre, and the lamps, hanging from the branches above, gave a gay, fantastic and fairy look to the scene. How often in such moments did I recall the lines of Goldsmith, describing those "kinder skies," beneath which "France displays her bright domain," and feel how true and masterly the sketch —

> Alike all ages; dames of ancient days
> Have led their children through the mirthful maze,
> And the gay grandsire, skilled in gestic lore,
> Has frisked beneath the burden of three-score.

Nor must I forget to mention the *Fête Patronale*, — a kind of annual fair, which is held at mid-summer in honor of the patron saint of Auteuil. Then the principal street of the village is filled with booths of every description; strolling players, and rope-dancers, and jugglers, and giants, and dwarfs, and wild beasts, and all kinds of wonderful shows excite the gaping curiosity of the throng, and in dust, crowds, and confusion the village rivals the capitalitself. Then the goodly dames of Passy descend into the village of Auteuil; — then the brewers of Billancourt, and the tanners of Sèvres dance lustily under the greenwood tree; — and then, too, the sturdy fishmongers of Brétigny and Saint-Yon regale their fat wives with an airing in a swing, and their customers with eels and craw-fish; — or as is more poetically set forth in an old Christmas Carol,

> Vous eussiez vu venir tous ceux de Saint-Yon,
> Et ceux de Brétigny apportant du poisson,
> Les barbeaux et gardons, anguilles et carpettes
> Etoient à bon marché
> Croyez,
> A cette journée-là,
> La, la,
> Et aussi les perchettes.

I found another source of amusement in observing the various personages that daily passed and repassed beneath my window. The character, which most of all arrested my attention, was a poor blind fiddler, whom I first saw chaunting a doleful ballad at the door of a small tavern near the gate of the village. He wore a brown coat out at elbows, the fragment of a velvet waistcoat, and a pair of tight nankeens, so short as hardly to reach below his calves. A little foraging cap, that had long since seen its best days, set off an open, good-humored countenance, bronzed by sun and wind. He was led about by a brisk middle aged woman, in straw hat and wooden shoes; and a little bare-footed boy, with clear blue eyes and flaxen hair, held a tattered hat in his hand, in which he collected eleemosynary sous. The old fellow had a favorite song, which he used to sing with great glee to a merry, joyous air, the burden of which ran *"chantons l'amour et le plaisir!"* — let us sing of love and pleasure. I often thought it would have been a good lesson for the crabbed and discontented rich man, to have heard this remnant of humanity, — poor, blind, and in rags, and dependent upon casual charity for his daily bread, singing, in so cheerful a voice, the charms of existence, and, as it were, fiddling life away to a merry tune.

I was one morning called to my window by the sound of rustic music. I looked out, and beheld a procession of villagers advancing along the road, attired in gay dresses, and marching merrily on in the direction of the church. I soon perceived that it was a marriage festival. The procession was led by a long orang-outang of a man, in a straw hat and white dimity bob-coat, playing on an asthmatic clarionet, from which he contrived to blow unearthly sounds, ever and anon squeaking off at right angles from his tune, and winding up with a grand flourish on the guttural notes. Behind him, led by his little boy, came the blind fiddler, his honest features glowing with all the hilarity of a rustic bridal, and, as he stumbled along, sawing away upon his fiddle till he made all crack again. Then came the happy bridegroom, dressed in his Sunday suit of blue, with a large nosegay in his button-hole, and close beside him his blushing bride, with downcast eyes, clad in a white robe and slippers, and wearing a wreath of white roses in her hair. The friends and relatives brought up the procession; and a troop of village urchins came shouting along in the rear, scrambling among themselves for the largess of sous and sugar-plums, that now and then issued in large handfuls from the pockets of a lean man in black, who seemed to officiate as master of ceremonies on the occasion. I gazed on the procession till it was out of sight; and when the last wheeze of the clarionet died upon my ear, I could not help thinking how happy were they, who were thus to dwell together in the peaceful bosom of their native village, far from the gilded misery and the pestilential vices of the town.

On the evening of the same day, I was sitting by the window, enjoying the freshness of the air, and the beauty and stillness of the hour, when I heard the distant and solemn hymn of the Catholic burial service, at first so faintly and indistinct that it seemed an illusion. It rose mournfully on the hush of evening, — died gradually away, — then ceased. Then it rose again, nearer and more distinct, and soon after a funeral procession appeared, and passed directly beneath my window. It was led by a priest, bearing the banner of the church, and followed by two boys, holding long flambeaux in their hands. Next came a double file of priests in white surplices, with a missal in one hand and a lighted wax taper in the other, chaunting the funeral dirge at intervals, — now pausing, and then again taking up the mournful burden of their lamentation, accompanied by others, who played upon a rude kind of horn, with a dismal and wailing sound. Then followed various symbols of the church, and the bier, borne on the shoulders of four men. The coffin was covered with a black velvet pall, and a chaplet of white flowers lay upon it, indicating that the deceased was unmarried. A few of the villagers came behind, clad in mourning robes, and bearing lighted tapers. The procession passed slowly along the same street, that in the morning had been thronged by the gay bridal company. A melancholy train of thought forced itself home upon my mind. The joys and sorrows of this world are so strikingly mingled! Our mirth and grief are brought so mournfully in contact! We laugh while others weep, — and others rejoice when we are sad! The light heart and the heavy walk side by side, and go about together! Beneath the same roof are spread the wedding feast and the funeral pall! The bridal song mingles with the burial hymn! One goes to the marriage bed; another to the grave; and all is mutable, uncertain and transitory!

It is with sensations of pure delight, that I recur to the brief period of my existence, which was passed in the peaceful shades of Auteuil. There is one kind of wisdom, which we learn from the world, and another kind, which can be acquired in solitude only. In cities we study those around us; but in the retirement of the country we learn to know ourselves. The voice within us is more distinctly audible in the stillness of the place; and the gentler affections of our nature spring up more freshly in its tranquillity and sunshine, — nurtured by the healthy principle, which we inhale with the pure air, and invigorated by the genial influences, which descend into the heart from the quiet of the sylvan solitude around, and the soft serenity of the sky above.

JACQUELINE.

When thou shalt see the body put on death's sad and ashy countenance, in the dead age of night, when silent darkness does encompass the dim light of thy glimmering taper, and thou hearest a solemn bell tolled to tell the world of it, which now, as it were, with this sound is struck into dumb attention, tell me if thou canst then find a thought of thine devoting thee to pleasure and the fugitive toys of life.

— Owen Felltham's Resolves.

JACQUELINE.

Death lies on her, like an untimely frost
Upon the sweetest flower of all the field.
— Shakspeare.

"Dear mother, — is it not the bell I hear?"

"Yes, my child; the bell for morning prayers. It is Sunday to-day."

"I had forgotten it. But now all days are alike to me. Hark! it sounds again — louder — louder. Open the window, for I love the sound. There; the sunshine and the fresh morning air revive me. And the church bell — oh mother, — it reminds me of the holy sabbath mornings by the Loire — so calm, so hushed, so beautiful! Now give me my prayer-book, and draw the curtain back that I may see the green trees and the church spire. I feel better to-day, dear mother."

It was a bright, cloudless morning in August. The dew still glistened on the trees; and a slight breeze wafted to the sick-chamber of Jacqueline the song of the birds, the rustle of the leaves, and the solemn chime of the church-bells. She had been raised up in bed, and reclining upon the pillow, was gazing wistfully upon the quiet scene without. Her mother gave her the prayer-book and then turned away to hide a tear that stole down her cheek.

At length the bells ceased. Jacqueline crossed herself, kissed a pearl crucifix that hung around her neck, and opened the silver clasps of her missal. For a time she seemed wholly absorbed in her devotions. Her lips moved, — but no sound was audible. At intervals the solemn voice of the priest was heard at a distance, and then the confused responses of the congregation, dying away in inarticulate murmurs. Ere long the thrilling chaunt of the Catholic service broke upon the ear. At first it was low, solemn, and indistinct; — then it became more earnest and entreating, as if interceding, and imploring pardon for sin; — and then arose louder and louder, full, harmonious, majestic, as it wafted the song of praise to heaven, — and suddenly ceased. Then the sweet tones of the organ were heard, — trembling, thrilling, and rising higher and higher, and filling the whole air with their rich melodious music. What exquisite accords! — what noble harmonies! — What touching pathos! — The soul of the sick girl seemed to kindle into more ardent devotion, and to be wrapt away to heaven in the full harmonious chorus, as it swelled onward, doubling and redoubling, and rolling upward in a full burst of rapturous devotion! — Then all was hushed again. Once more the low sound of the bell smote the air, and announced the elevation of the host. The invalid seemed entranced in prayer. Her book had fallen beside her, — her hands were clasped, — her eyes closed, — her soul retired within its secret chambers. Then a more triumphant peal of bells arose. The tears gushed from her closed and swollen lids; her cheek was flushed; she opened her dark eyes and fixed them with an expression of deep adoration and penitence upon an image of the Savior on the cross, which hung at the foot of her bed, and her lips again moved in prayer. Her countenance expressed the deepest resignation. She seemed to ask only that she might die in peace, and go to the bosom of her Redeemer.

The mother was kneeling by the window, with her face concealed in the folds of the curtain. She arose, and, going to the bedside of her child, threw her arms around her, and burst into tears.

"My dear mother, I shall not live long — I feel it here. This piercing pain — at times it seizes me, and I cannot — cannot breathe."

"My child, you will be better soon."

"Yes, mother, I shall be better soon. All tears and pain and sorrow will be over. The hymn of adoration and entreaty I have just heard, I shall never hear again on earth. Next sabbath, mother, kneel again by that window as to-day. I shall not be here, upon this bed of pain and sickness, but when you hear the solemn hymn of worship and the beseeching tones that wing the spirit up to God, think, mother, that I am there, — with my sweet sister who has gone before us, — kneeling at our Savior's feet, and happy — oh, how happy!"

The afflicted mother made no reply, — her heart was too full to speak.

"You remember, mother, how calmly Amie died. Poor child, she was so young and beautiful! — I always pray, that I may die as she did. I do not fear death as I did before she was taken from us. But oh — this pain — this cruel pain — it seems to draw my mind back from heaven. When it leaves me I shall die in peace."

"My poor child! — God's holy will be done!"

The invalid soon sank into a quiet slumber. The excitement was over, and exhausted nature sought relief in sleep.

The persons, between whom this scene passed, were a widow and her sick daughter, from the neighborhood of Tours. They had left the banks of the Loire to consult the more experienced physicians of the metropolis, and had been directed to the *Maison de*

Santé at Auteuil for the benefit of the pure air. But all in vain. The health of the suffering, but uncomplaining patient grew worse and worse, and it soon became evident that the closing scene was drawing near.

Of this Jacqueline herself seemed conscious; and toward evening she expressed a wish to receive the last sacraments of the church. A priest was sent for: and ere long the tinkling of a little bell in the street announced his approach. He bore in his hand a silver vase containing the consecrated wafer, and a small vessel filled with the holy oil of the extreme unction hung from his neck. Before him walked a boy carrying a little bell, whose sound announced the passing of these symbols of the Catholic faith. In the rear, a few of the villagers, bearing lighted wax tapers, formed a short and melancholy procession. They soon entered the sick chamber, and the glimmer of the tapers mingled with the red light of the setting sun, that shot his farewell rays through the open window. The vessel of oil and the vase containing the consecrated wafers were placed upon the table in front of a crucifix, that hung upon the wall, and all present excepting the priest, threw themselves upon their knees. The priest then approached the bed of the dying girl, and said in a slow and solemn tone;

"The King of kings and Lord of lords has passed thy threshold. Is thy spirit ready to receive him?" —

"It is, father."

"Hast thou confessed thy sins?"

"Holy father, no."

"Confess thyself, then, that thy sins may be forgiven, and thy name recorded in the book of life."

And turning to the kneeling crowd around, he waved his hand for them to retire, and was left alone with the sick girl. He seated himself beside her pillow, and the subdued whisper of the confession mingled with the murmur of the evening air, which lifted the heavy folds of the curtains and stole in upon the holy scene. Poor Jacqueline had few sins to confess, — a secret thought or two towards the pleasures and delights of the world, — a wish to live, unuttered, but which to the eye of her self-accusing spirit seemed to resist the wise providence of God; — no more. The confession of a meek and lowly heart is soon made. The door was again opened; — the attendants entered, and knelt around the bed, and the priest proceeded;

"And now prepare thyself to receive with contrite heart the body of our blessed Lord and Redeemer. — Dost thou believe that our Lord Jesus Christ was conceived by the Holy Spirit, and born of the Virgin Mary?"

"I believe."

And all present joined in the solemn response —

"I believe."

"Dost thou believe that the Father is God, that the Son is God, and that the Holy Spirit is God, — three persons and one God?"

"I believe."

"Dost thou believe that the Son is seated on the right hand of the Majesty on high, whence he shall come to judge the quick and the dead?"

"I believe."

"Dost thou believe that by the holy sacraments of the church thy sins are forgiven thee, and that thus thou art made worthy of eternal life?" "I believe."

"Dost thou pardon, with all thy heart, all who have offended thee in thought, word or deed?"

"I pardon them."

"And dost thou ask pardon of God and thy neighbor for all offences thou hast committed against them, either in thought, word, or deed?"

"I do!"

"Then repeat after me; O Lord Jesus, I am not worthy, nor do I merit, that thy divine Majesty should enter this poor tenement of clay; but according to thy holy promises be my sins forgiven, and my soul washed white from all transgression."

Then taking a consecrated wafer from the vase, he placed it between the lips of the dying girl, and while the assistant sounded the little silver bell, said;

"*Corpus Domini nostri Jesu Christi custodiat animam tuam in vitam eternam.*"

And the kneeling crowd smote their breasts and responded in one solemn voice;

"Amen!"

The priest then took from the silver box on the table a little golden rod, and dipping it in holy oil, anointed the invalid upon the hands, feet and breast in the form of the cross. When these ceremonies were completed, the priest and his attendants retired, leaving the mother alone with her dying child, who, from the exhaustion caused by the preceding scene, sank into a death-like sleep.

> '*Between two worlds life hovered like a star,*
> '*Twixt night and morn upon the horizon's verge.*'

The long twilight of the summer evening stole on; the shadows deepened without, and the night-lamp glimmered feebly in the sick chamber; but still she slept. She was lying with her hands clasped upon her breast, — her pallid cheek resting upon the pillow, and her bloodless lips apart, but motionless and silent as the sleep of death. Not a breath interrupted the silence of her slumber. Not a movement of the heavy and sunken eye-lid-not a trembling of the lip — not a shadow on the marble brow told when the spirit took its flight. It passed to a better world than this.

> 'There's a perpetual spring, — perpetual youth;
> No joint-benumbing cold, nor scorching heat,
> Famine, nor age have any being there.'

THE SEXAGENARIAN,
A SKETCH OF CHARACTER.

Youth is full of pleasure,
Age is full of care;
Youth like summer morn,
Age like winter weather;
Youth like summer brave,
Age like winter bare;
Youth is full of sport,
Age's breath is short;
Youth is nimble, age is lame;
Youth is hot and bold,
Age is weak and cold;
Youth is wild, and age is tame.

— Shakspeare.

THE SEXAGENARIAN.

Do you set down your name in the scroll of youth, that are written down old, with all the characters of age? Have you not a moist eye? a dry hand? a yellow cheek? a white beard? a decreasing leg?

— Shakspeare.

There he goes, — in his long russet surtout, — sweeping down yonder gravel walk beneath the trees, like a yellow leaf in Autumn, wafted along by a fitful gust of wind. Now he pauses; — now seems to be whirled round in an eddy, — and now rustles and brushes onward again. He is talking to himself in an undertone as usual; and flourishes a pinch of snuff between his fore-finger and his thumb, — ever and anon drumming on the cover of his box by way of emphasis, with a sound like the tap of a wood-pecker. He always takes a morning walk in the garden, — in fact, I may say he passes a greater part of the day there, either strolling up and down the gravel walks, or sitting on a rustic bench in one of the leafy arbors. He always wears that same dress, too; at least, I have never seen him in any other; — a bell-crowned hat, — a frilled bosom, and white dimity vest, soiled with snuff, — light nankeen smalls, — and, over all, that long and flowing surtout of russet-brown circassian, hanging in wrinkles round his slender body, and toying with his thin rakish legs. Such is his constant garb, morning and evening; and it gives him a cool and breezy look even in the heat of a noon-day in August.

The personage, sketched in the preceding paragraph, is Monsieur D'Argentville, a sexagenarian, with whom I became acquainted during my residence at the *Maison de Santé* of Auteuil. I found him there, and left him there. No body knew when he came, — he had been there from time immemorial; nor when he was going away, — for he himself did not know; — nor what ailed him, — for though he was always complaining, yet he grew neither better nor worse, never consulted the physician, and ate voraciously three times a day. At table he was rather peevish, troubled his neighbors with his elbows, and uttered the monosyllable pish! rather oftener than good-breeding and a due deference to the opinions of others seemed to justify. As soon as he seated himself at table he breathed into his tumbler, and wiped it out with a napkin; then wiped his plate, his spoon, his knife and fork, in succession, and each with great care. After this he placed the napkin under his chin, by way of bib and tucker, and, these preparations being completed, gave full swing to an appetite, which was not inappropriately denominated, by one of our guests, *une faim canine.*

The old gentleman's weak side was an affectation of youth and gallantry. Though "written down old, with all the characters of age," yet at times he seemed to think himself in the hey-day of life; and the assiduous court he paid to a fair Countess, who was passing the summer at the *Maison de Santé*, was the source of no little merriment to all but himself. He loved, too, to recall the golden age of his amours; and would discourse with prolix eloquence, and a faint twinkle in his watery eye, of his *bonnes fortunes* in times of old, and the rigors, that many a fair dame had suffered on his account. Indeed, his chief pride seemed to be to make his hearers believe, that he had been a dangerous man in his youth, and was not yet quite safe.

As I also was a peripatetic of the garden, we encountered each other at every turn. At first our conversation was limited to the usual salutations of the day; but ere long our casual acquaintance ripened into a kind of intimacy. Step by step I won my way, — first into his society, — then into his snuff-box, — and then into his heart. He was a great talker, and he found in me, what he found in no other inmate of the house, — a good listener, who never interrupted his long stories, nor contradicted his opinions. So he talked down one alley and up another, — from breakfast till dinner, — from dinner till midnight; — at all times and in all places, when he could catch me by the button, till at last he had confided to my ear all the important and unimportant events of a life of sixty years. Monsieur D'Argentville was a shoot from a wealthy family of Nantes. Just before the Revolution he went up to Paris to study law at the University; and like many other wealthy scholars of his age, was soon involved in the intrigues and dissipation of the metropolis. He first established himself in the Rue de l'Université; but a roguish pair of eyes, at an opposite window, soon drove from the field such heavy tacticians as Hugues Doneau and Gui Coquille. A flirtation was commenced in due form; and a flag of truce, offering to capitulate, was sent in the shape of a billet-doux. In the mean time he regularly amused his leisure hours by blowing kisses across the street with an old pair of bellows. One afternoon, as he was occupied in this way, a tall gentleman with whiskers stepped into the room, just as he had charged the bellows to the muzzle. He muttered something about an explanation — his sister — marriage — and the satisfaction of a gentleman! Perhaps there is no situation in life so awkward to a man of real sensibility, as that of being awed into matrimony or a duel by the whiskers of a tall brother. There was but one alternative; and the next morning a placard at the window of the Bachelor of Love, with the words "Furnished Appartment to let," showed that the former occupant had found it convenient to change lodgings.

He next appeared in the Chaussée-d'Antin, where he assiduously prepared himself for future exigencies, by a course of daily lessons in the use of the small-sword. He soon after quarrelled with his best friend, about a little actress on the Boulevard, and had the satisfaction of being jilted, and then run through the body at the Bois de Boulogne. This gave him new eclat in the fashionable world; and consequently he pursued pleasure with a keener relish than ever. He next had the grande passion, and narrowly escaped marrying an heiress of great expectations, and a countless number of chateaux. Just before the catastrophe, however, he had the good fortune to discover, that the lady's expectations were limited to his own pocket, and that as for her chateaux, they were all *Chateaux en Espagne.*

About this time his father died; and the hopeful son was hardly well established in his inheritance, when the Revolution broke out. Unfortunately he was a firm upholder of the divine right of kings, and had the honor of being among the first of the proscribed. He narrowly escaped the guillotine by jumping on board a vessel bound for America, and arrived at Boston with only a few francs in his pocket; but as he knew how to accommodate himself to circumstances, he continued to live along by teaching fencing and French, and keeping a dancing-school and a milliner.

At the restoration of the Bourbons he returned to France; and from that time to the day of our acquaintance had been engaged in a series of vexatious law-suits, in the hope of recovering a portion of his property, which had been entrusted to a friend for safe keeping, at the commencement of the Revolution. His friend, however, denied all knowledge of the transaction, and the assignment was very difficult to prove. Twelve years of unsuccessful litigation had completely soured the old gentleman's temper, and made him peevish and misanthropic; and he had come to Auteuil, merely to escape the noise of the city, and to brace his shattered nerves with pure air and quiet amusements. There he idled the time away, sauntering about the garden of the *Maison de Santé*, talking to himself, when he could get no other listener, and occasionally reinforcing his misanthropy with a dose of the Maxims of La Rochefoucauld, or a visit to the scene of his duel in the Bois de

Bologne.

Poor Monsieur D'Argentville! What a miserable life he led —
or rather dragged on from day to day! — A petulant, broken-down
old man, who had outlived his fortune, and his friends, and his
hopes, — yea, every thing but the sting of bad passions, and the
recollection of a life ill-spent! — Whether he still walks the earth,
or slumbers in its bosom, I know not; but a lively recollection of
him will always mingle with my reminiscences of Auteuil.

PÈRE LA CHAISE.

Death levels all things in his march;
Nought can resist his mighty strength;
The palace proud, — triumphal arch,
Shall mete their shadow's length.
The rich, the poor, one common bed
Shall find in the unhonoured grave,
Where weeds shall crown alike the head
Of tyrant and of slave.

— Marvel.

PÈRE LA CHAISE.

*Our fathers find their graves in our short memories, and
sadly tell us how we may be buried in our survivors.*

*Oblivion is not to be hired. The greater part must be con-
tent to be as though they had not been, to be found in the reg-
ister of God, not in the record of man.*

— Sir Thomas Brown's Urn-Burial.

The cemetery of Père La Chaise is the Westminster Abbey of
Paris. Both are the dwellings of the dead; but in one they repose in
green alleys and beneath the open sky; — in the other their resting
place is in the shadowy aisle and beneath the dim arches of an
ancient abbey. One is a temple of nature — the other a temple of
art. In one the soft melancholy of the scene is rendered still more
touching by the warble of birds and the shade of trees, and the
grave receives the gentle visit of the sunshine and the shower; — in
the other no sound but the passing foot-fall breaks the silence of
the place; the twilight steals in through high and dusky windows;
and the damps of the gloomy vault lie heavy on the heart, and
leave their stain upon the mouldering tracery of the tomb.

Père La Chaise stands just beyond the *Barrière d' Aulney*, on a
hill side, looking towards the city. Numerous gravel walks, winding through shady avenues and between marble monuments, lead
up from the principal entrance to a chapel on the summit. There is
hardly a grave that has not its little enclosure planted with shrubbery; and a thick mass of foliage half conceals each funeral stone.
The sighing of the wind, as the branches rise and fall upon it, —
the occasional note of a bird among the trees, and the shifting of
light and shade upon the tombs beneath, have a soothing effect
upon the mind; and I doubt whether any one can enter that enclosure, where repose the dust and ashes of so many great and good
men, without feeling the religion of the place steal over him, and
seeing something of the dark and gloomy expression pass off from
the stern countenance of death.

It was near the close of a bright summer afternoon, that I visited this celebrated spot for the first time. The first object, that
arrested my attention on entering, was a monument in the form of
a small gothic chapel, which stands near the entrance, in the
avenue leading to the right hand. On the marble couch within are
stretched two figures carved in stone, and dressed in the antique
garb of the Middle Ages. It is the tomb of Abélard and Héloïse.
The history of these unfortunate lovers is too well known to need
recapitulation; but perhaps it is not so well known how often their

ashes were disturbed in the slumber of the grave. Abélard died in the monastery of Saint-Marcel, and was buried in the vaults of the church. His body was afterwards removed to the convent of the Paraclet, at the request of Héloïse, and at her death her body was deposited in the same tomb. Three centuries they reposed together; after which they were separated to different sides of the church to calm the delicate scruples of the lady Abbess of the convent. More than a century afterwards, they were again united in the same tomb; and when at length the Paraclet was destroyed, their mouldering remains were transported to the church of Nogent-sur-Seine. They were next deposited in an ancient cloister at Paris; and now repose near the gate-way of the cemetery of Père La Chaise. What a singular destiny was theirs! — that after a life of such passionate and disastrous love — such sorrows, and tears, and penitence — their very dust should not be suffered to rest quietly in the grave! that their death should so much resemble their life in its changes and vicissitudes — its partings and its meetings, — its inquietudes and its persecutions! that mistaken zeal should follow them down to the very tomb, — as if earthly passion could glimmer, like a funeral lamp, amid the damps of the charnel-house, and "even in their ashes burn their wonted fires!"

As I gazed on the sculptured forms before me, and the little chapel, whose gothic roof seemed to protect their marble sleep, my busy memory swung back the dark portals of the past, and the picture of their sad and eventful lives came up before me in the gloomy distance. What a lesson for those who are endowed with the fatal gift of genius! — It would seem, indeed, that he who "tempers the wind to the shorn lamb," tempers also his chastisements to the errors and infirmities of a weak and simple mind, — while the transgressions of him upon whose nature are more strongly marked the intellectual attributes of the deity, are followed, even upon earth, by severer tokens of the divine displeasure. He who sins in the darkness of a benighted intellect, sees not so clearly, through the shadows that surround him, the countenance of an offended God; — but he who sins in the broad noonday of a clear and radiant mind, when at length the delirium of sensual passion has subsided, and the cloud flits away from before the sun, trembles beneath the searching eye of that accusing power, which is strong in the strength of a godlike intellect. Thus the mind and the heart are closely linked together, and the errors of genius bear with them their own chastisement, even upon earth. The history of Abélard and Héloïse is an illustration of this truth. But at length they sleep well. Their lives are like a tale that is told; their errors are "folded up like a book;" and what mortal hand shall break the seal that death has set upon them!

Leaving this interesting tomb behind me, I took a path-way to the left which conducted me up the hill-side. I soon found myself in the deep shade of heavy foliage, where the branches of the yew and willow mingled, interwoven with the tendrils and blossoms of the honey-suckle. I now stood in the most populous part of this city of tombs. Every step awakened a new train of thrilling recollections; for at every step my eye caught the name of some one, whose glory had exalted the character of his native land, and resounded across the waters of the Atlantic. Philosophers, historians, musicians, warriors, and poets slept side by side around me; some beneath the gorgeous monument, and some beneath the simple head-stone. There were the graves of Fourcroi and Haüy; — of Ginguené and Volney; — of Grêtry and Méhul; — of Ney, and Foy, and Masséna; — of La Fontaine, and Molière, and Chénier, and Delille, and Parny. But the political intrigue, the dream of science, the historical research, the ravishing harmony of sound, the tried courage, the inspiration of the lyre, — where are they? With the living, and not with the dead! The right hand has lost its cunning in the grave; but the soul, whose high volitions it obeyed, still lives to reproduce itself in ages yet to come.

Among these graves of genius, I observed here and there a splendid monument, which had been raised by the pride of family, over the dust of men, who could lay no claim either to the gratitude or remembrance of posterity. Their presence seemed like an intrusion into the sanctuary of genius. What had wealth to do there? Why should it crowd the dust of the great! That was no thoroughfare of business — no mart of gain! There were no costly banquets there; no silken garments, nor gaudy liveries, nor obsequious attendants! "What servants," says Jeremy Taylor, "shall we have to wait upon us in the grave? What friends to visit us? What officious people to cleanse away the moist and unwholesome cloud reflected upon our faces from the sides of the weeping vaults, which are the longest weepers for our funerals?" Material wealth gives a factitious superiority to the living, but the treasures of intellect give a real superiority to the dead; and the rich man, who would not deign to walk the street with the starving and penniless man of genius, deems it an honor, when death has redeemed the fame of the neglected, to have his own ashes laid beside him, and to claim with him the silent companionship of the grave.

I continued my walk through the numerous winding paths, as

chance or curiosity directed me. Now I was lost in a little green hollow, overhung with thick-leaved shrubbery, and then came out upon an elevation, from which, through an opening in the trees, the eye caught glimpses of the city, and the little esplanade at the foot of the hill, where the poor lie buried. There poverty hires its grave, and takes but a short lease of the narrow house. At the end of a few months, or at most of a few years, the tenant is dislodged to give place to another, and he in turn to a third. "Who," says Sir Thomas Browne, "knows the fate of his bones, or how often he is to be buried? who hath the oracle of his ashes, or whither they are to be scattered?"

Yet, even in that neglected corner, the hand of affection had been busy in decorating the hired house. Most of the graves were surrounded with a slight wooden paling, to secure them from the passing footstep; — there was hardly one so deserted as not to be marked with its little wooden cross, and decorated with a garland of flowers; and here and there I could perceive a solitary mourner, clothed in black, stooping to plant a shrub on the grave, or sitting in motionless sorrow beside it.

As I passed on amid the shadowy avenues of the cemetery, I could not help comparing my own impressions, with those which others have felt when walking alone among the dwellings of the dead. Are, then, the sculptured urn and storied monument nothing more than symbols of family pride? Is all I see around me a memorial of the living more than of the dead? — an empty show of sorrow, which thus vaunts itself in mournful pageant and funeral parade? Is it indeed true, as some have said, that the simple wild-flower, which springs spontaneously upon the grave, and the rose, which the hand of affection plants there, are fitter objects wherewith to adorn the narrow house? No! — I feel that it is not so! Let the good and the great be honored even in the grave. Let the sculptured marble direct our footsteps to the scene of their long sleep; let the chiselled epitaph repeat their names, and tell us where repose the nobly good and wise! It is not true that all are equal in the grave. There is no equality even there. The mere handful of dust and ashes — the mere distinction of prince and beggar — of a rich winding-sheet and a shroudless burial — of a solitary grave and a family vault — were this all — then indeed it would be true that death is a common leveller. Such paltry distinctions as those of wealth and poverty are soon levelled by the spade and mattoc; the damp breath of the grave blots them out forever. But there are other distinctions which even the mace of death cannot level or obliterate. Can it break down the distinction of virtue and vice? Can it confound the good with the bad? the noble with the base? all that is truly great, and pure and godlike, with all that is scorned, and sinful, and degraded! No! Then death is not a common leveller! Are all alike beloved in death and honored in their burial? Is that ground holy where the bloody hand of the murderer sleeps from crime? Does every grave awaken the same emotions in our hearts? and do the foot-steps of the stranger pause as long beside each funeral stone? No! Then all are not equal in the grave! And as long as the good and evil deeds of men live after them, so long will there be distinctions even in the grave. The superiority of one over another is in the nobler and better emotions which it excites; in its more fervent admonitions to virtue; in the livelier recollection, which it awakens, of the good and the great, whose bodies are crumbling to dust beneath our feet!

If, then, there are distinctions in the grave, surely it is not unwise to designate them by the external marks of honor. These outward appliances and memorials of respect, — the mournful urn, — the sculptured bust, — the epitaph eloquent in praise, — cannot indeed create these distinctions, but they serve to mark them. It is only when pride or wealth builds them to honor the slave of mammon, or the slave of appetite, when the voice from the grave rebukes the false and pompous epitaph, and the dust and ashes of the tomb seem struggling to maintain the superiority of mere worldly rank, and to carry into the grave the baubles of earthly vanity, — it is then, and then only, that we feel how utterly worthless are all the devices of sculpture, and the empty pomp of monumental brass!

After rambling leisurely about for some time, reading the inscriptions on the various monuments, which attracted my curiosity, and giving way to the different reflections they suggested, I sat down to rest myself on a sunken tombstone. A winding gravel-walk, overshaded by an avenue of trees, and lined on both sides with richly sculptured monuments, had gradually conducted me to the summit of the hill, upon whose slope the cemetery stands. Beneath me in the distance, and dim-discovered through the misty and smoky atmosphere of evening, rose the countless roofs and spires of the city. Beyond, throwing his level rays athwart the dusky landscape, sank the broad red sun. The distant murmur of the city rose upon my ear; and the toll of the evening bell came up, mingled with the rattle of the paved street and the confused sounds of labor. What an hour for meditation! What a contrast between the metropolis of the living and the metropolis of the dead! I could not help calling to my mind that allegory of mortality, written by a hand, which has been many a long year cold;

Earth goeth upon earth as man upon mould,
Like as earth upon earth never go should,
Earth goeth upon earth as glistening gold,
And yet shall earth unto earth rather than he would.
Lo, earth on earth, consider thou may,
How earth cometh to earth naked alway,
Why shall earth upon earth go stout or gay,
Since earth out of earth shall pass in poor array.[2]

2   I subjoin this relic of old English verse entire, and in its antiquated language, for those of my readers, who may have an antiquarian taste. It is copied from a book, whose title I have forgotten, and of which I have but a single leaf, containing the poem. In describing the antiquities of the church of Stratford-upon-Avon, the writer gives the following account of a very old painting upon the wall, and of the poem, which served as its motto. The painting is no longer visible, having been effaced in repairing the church.

"Against the west wall of the nave, on the south side of the arch, was painted the martyrdom of Thomas-a-Becket, whilst kneeling at the altar of St. Benedict in Canterbury cathedral; below this was the figure of an angel, probably St. Michael, supporting a long scroll, upon which were seven stanzas in old English, being an allegory of mortality;

Erthe oute of erthe ys wondurly wroght
Erth hath gotyn uppon erth a dygnyte of noght
Erth ypon erth hath sett all hys thowht
How erth apon erth may be hey browght

Erth upon erth wold be a kyng
But how that erth gott to erth he thyngkys nothyng
When erth byddys erth hys rentys whom bryng
Then schall erth apon erth have a hard ptyng

Erth apon erth wynnys castellys and towrys
Then seth erth unto erth thys ys all owrys
When erth apon eath hath bylde hys bowrys
Then schall erth for erth suffur many hard schowrys

Erth goth apon erth as man apon mowld
Lyke as erth apon erth never goo schold
Erth goth apon erth as gelsteryng gold

Before I left the grave-yard, the shades of evening had fallen, and the objects around me grown dim and indistinct. As I passed the gate-way, I turned to take a parting look. I could distinguish only the chapel on the summit of the hill, and here and there a lofty obelisk of snow-white marble, rising from the black and heavy mass of foliage around, and pointing upward to the gleam of the departed sun, that still lingered in the sky, and mingled with the soft star-light of a summer evening.

And yet schall erth unto erth rather then he wold

Why that erth loveth erth wondur me thynke
Or why that erth wold for erth other swett or swynke
When erth apon erth ys broght wt.yn the brynke
Then schall erth apon erth have a fowll stynke

Lo erth on erth consedur thow may
How erth comyth to erth nakyd all way
Why schall erth apon erth goo stowte or gay
Seth erth owt of erth schall passe yn poor aray

I counsill erth apon erth that ys wondurly wrogt
The whyl yt. erth ys apon erth to torne hys thowht
And pray to god upon erth yt. all erth wroght
That all crystyn soullys to ye. blys.may be broght

Beneath were two men, holding a scroll over a body wrapt in a winding sheet, and covered with some emblems of mortality; etc."

VOLUME 2

I have passed manye landes and manye yles and con-trees, and cherched manye fulle straunge places, and have ben in manye a fulle gode honourable companye. Now I am comen home to reste. And thus recordynge the tyme passed, I have fulfilled these thynges and putte hem wryten in this boke, as it woulde come into my mynde.

— Sir John Maundeville.

THE VALLEY OF THE LOIRE.

Je ne conçois qu'une manière de voyager plus agréable que d'aller à cheval; c'est d'aller à pied. On part à son moment, on s'arrête à sa volonté, on fait tant et si pen d'exercise qu'on veut.

Quand on ne veut qu'arriver, on peut courir en chaise de poste; mais quand on veut voyager, il fant aller à pied.

— Rousseau.

THE VALLEY OF THE LOIRE.

Beside the murmuring Loire,
Where shading elms along the margin grew,
And freshened from the wave the zephyr flew.
— Goldsmith.

In the melancholy month of October I made a foot-excursion along the banks of the Loire, from Orleans to Tours. This luxuriant region is justly called the Garden of France. From Orleans to Blois the whole valley of the Loire is one continued vineyard. The bright green foliage of the vine spreads, like the undulations of the sea, over all the landscape; with here and there a silver flash of the river, — a sequestered hamlet, — or the towers of an old chateau, to enliven and variegate the scene.

The vintage had already commenced. The peasantry were busy in the fields, — the song that cheered their labor was on the breeze, and the heavy wagon tottered by, laden with the clusters of the vine. Every thing around me wore that happy look, which makes the heart glad. In the morning I arose with the lark; and at night I slept where sunset overtook me. The healthy exercise of foot-travelling, — the pure, bracing air of Autumn, and the cheerful aspect of the whole landscape about me, gave fresh elasticity to a mind not over-burdened with care, and made me forget, not only the fatigue of walking, but also the consciousness of being alone.

My first day's journey brought me at evening to a village, whose name I have forgotten, situated about eight leagues from Orleans. It is a small, obscure hamlet, not mentioned in the guide-book, and stands upon the precipitous banks of a deep ravine, through which a noisy brook leaps down to turn the ponderous wheel of a thatch-roofed mill. The village inn stands upon the high-way; but the village itself is not visible to the traveller as he passes. It is completely hidden in the lap of a wooded valley; and so embowered in trees, that not a roof nor a chimney peeps out to betray its hiding place. It is like the nest of a ground-swallow, which the passing footstep almost treads upon, and yet it is not seen. I passed by without suspecting, that a village was near; and the little inn had a look so uninviting, that I did not even enter it.

After proceeding a mile or two farther, I perceived, upon my left, a village spire, rising over the vineyards. Towards this I directed my footsteps; but it seemed to recede as I advanced, and at last quite disappeared. It was evidently many miles distant; and as the path I followed descended from the highway, it had gradually sunk beneath a swell of the vine-clad landscape. I now found myself in the midst of an extensive vineyard. It was just sunset; and the last golden rays lingered on the rich and mellow scenery around me. The peasantry were still busy at their task; and the occasional bark of a dog, and the distant sound of an evening bell gave fresh romance to the scene. The reality of many a day-dream of childhood, — of many a poetic revery of youth was before me. I stood at sunset amid the luxuriant vineyards of France!

The first person I met was a poor old woman, a little bowed down with age, gathering grapes into a large basket. She was dressed like the poorest class of peasantry; and pursued her solitary task alone, heedless of the cheerful gossip, and the merry laugh, which came from a band of more youthful vintagers, at a short distance from her. She was so intently engaged in her work, that she did not perceive my approach, until I bade her good evening. On hearing my voice, she looked up from her labor, and returned the salutation: and on my asking her if there were a tavern, or a farm-house in the neighborhood, where I could pass the night, she showed me the pathway through the vineyard, that led to the village, and then added, with a look of curiosity;

"You must be a stranger, Sir, in these parts."

"Yes; my home is very far from here."

"How far?"

"More than a thousand leagues."

The old woman looked incredulous.

"I came from a distant land, beyond the sea."

"More than a thousand leagues!" at length repeated she; "And why have you come so far from home?"

"To travel; — to see how you live in this country."

"Have you no relations in your own?"

"Yes; I have both brothers and sisters; a father, and —"

"And a mother?"

"Thank heaven, I have."

"And did you leave her!"

Here the old woman gave me a piercing look of reproof; shook her head mournfully, and, with a deep sigh, as if some painful recollection had been awakened in her bosom, turned again to her solitary task. I felt rebuked; for there is something almost prophetic in the admonitions of the old. The eye of age looks meekly into my heart! the voice of age echoes mournfully through it! the hoary head and palsied hand of age plead irresistibly for its sympathies! I venerate old age; and I love not the man, who can look without emotion upon the sundown of life, when the dusk of evening begins to gather over the watery eye, and the shadows of twilight grow broader and deeper upon the understanding!

I pursued the path-way which led toward the village, and the next person I encountered was an old man stretched lazily beneath the vines upon a little strip of turf, at a point where four paths met, forming a cross-way in the vineyard. He was clad in a coarse garb of gray, with a pair of long gaiters or spatter-dashes. Beside him lay a blue cloth cap, a staff, and an old weather-beaten knapsack. I saw at once, that he was a foot-traveller like myself, and, therefore, without more ado, entered into conversation with him. From his language, and the peculiar manner in which he now and then wiped his upper lip with the back of his hand, as if in search of the mustache, which was no longer there, I judged that he had been a soldier. In this opinion I was not mistaken. He had served under Napoleon, and had followed the imperial eagle across the Alps, and the Pyrenees, and the burning sands of Egypt. Like every vieux moustache, he spake with enthusiasm of the Little Corporal, and cursed the English, the Germans, the Spanish, and every other race on earth, except the great nation — his own.

"I like," said he, "after a long day's march, to lie down in this way upon the grass, and enjoy the cool of the evening. It reminds me of the bivouacs of other days, and of old friends, who are now up there."

Here he pointed with his finger to the sky.

"They have reached the last *étape* before me, in the long march. But I shall go soon. We shall all meet again at the last roll-call. A soldier has a heart, — and can feel like other men. *Sacré nom de* —! There's a tear!"

He wiped it away with his sleeve.

Here our colloquy was interrupted by the approach of a group of vintagers, who were returning homeward from their labor. To this party I joined myself, and invited the old soldier to do the same; but he shook his head.

"I thank you; my path-way lies in a different direction."

"But there is no other village near, and the sun has already set."

"No matter. I am used to sleeping on the ground. Good night."

I left the old man to his meditations, and walked on in company with the vintagers. Following a well-trodden path-way through the vineyards, we soon descended the valley's slope, and I suddenly found myself in the bosom of one of those little hamlets, from which the laborer rises to his toil, as the sky-lark to his song. My companions wished me a good night, as each entered his own thatch-roofed cottage, — and a little girl led me out to the very inn, which an hour or two before, I had disdained to enter.

When I awoke in the morning, a brilliant Autumnal sun was shining in at my window. The merry song of birds mingled sweetly with the sound of rustling leaves, and the gurgle of the brook. The vintagers were going forth to their toil; the wine-press was busy in the shade, and the clatter of the mill kept time to the miller's song. I loitered about the village with a feeling of calm delight. I was unwilling to leave the seclusion of this sequestered hamlet; — but at length, with reluctant step, I took the cross-road through the vineyard, and in a moment the little village had sunk again, as if by enchantment, into the bosom of the earth.

I breakfasted at the town of Mer; and leaving the high-road to Blois on the right, passed down to the banks of the Loire, through a long, broad avenue of poplars and sicamores. I crossed the river in a boat, and in the after part of the day, found myself before the high and massive walls of the chateau of Chambord. This chateau is one of the finest specimens of the ancient Gothic castle to be found in Europe. The little river Cosson fills its deep and ample moat, and above it, the huge towers and heavy battlements rise in stern and solemn grandeur, moss-grown with age, and blackened by the storms of three centuries. Within, all is mournful and deserted. The grass has overgrown the pavement of the court-yard, — and the rude sculpture upon the walls is broken and defaced. From the court-yard I entered the central tower, and ascending the principal stair-case, went out upon the battlements. I seemed to have stepped back into the precincts of the feudal ages; and as I passed along through echoing corridors, and vast, deserted halls, stripped of their furniture, and mouldering silently away, the distant past came back upon me, and the times when the clang of arms, and the tramp of mail-clad men, and the sounds of music, and revelry and wassail echoed along those high-vaulted and solitary chambers!

My third day's journey brought me to the ancient city of Blois, the chief town of the department of Loire-et-Cher. This city is celebrated for the purity with which even the lower classes of its inhabitants speak their native tongue. It rises precipitously from the northern bank of the Loire; and many of its streets are so steep as to be almost impassible for carriages. On the brow of the hill, overlooking the roofs of the city, and commanding a fine view of the Loire and its noble bridge, and the surrounding country, sprinkled with cottages and country-seats, runs an ample terrace, planted with trees, and laid out as a public walk. The view from this terrace is one of the most beautiful in France. But what most strikes the eye of the traveller at Blois is an old, though still unfinished chateau. Its huge parapets of hewn stone stand upon either side of the street; but they have walled up the wide gate-way, from which the colossal draw-bridge was to have sprung high in air, connecting together the main towers of the chateau, and the two hills, upon whose slope its foundations stand. The aspect of the vast pile is gloomy and desolate. It seems as if the strong hand of the builder had been arrested in the midst of his task by the stronger hand of death; and the unfinished fabric stands a lasting monument both of the power and weakness of man, — of his vast desires, — his sanguine hopes, — his ambitious purposes, — and of the unlooked-for conclusion, where all these desires, and hopes, and purposes are so often arrested. — There is also at Blois another ancient chateau, to which some historic interest is attached, as being the scene of the massacre of the Duke of Guise.

On the following day I left Blois for Amboise, and after walking several leagues along the dusty highway, crossed the river in a boat to the little village of Moines, which lies amid luxuriant vineyards upon the southern bank of the Loire. From Moines to Amboise the road is truly delightful. The rich lowland scenery by the margin of the river is verdant even in October; and occasionally the landscape is diversified with the picturesque cottages of the vintagers, cut in the rock along the road-side, and overhung by the thick foliage of the vines above them.

At Amboise I took a cross-road, which led me to the romantic borders of the Cher, and the chateau of Chernanceau. This beautiful chateau, as well as that of Chambord, was built by the gay and munificent Francis the First. One is a specimen of strong and massive architecture — a dwelling for a warrior; — but the other is of a lighter and more graceful construction, and was destined for those soft languishments of passion, with which the fascinating Diane de Poitiers had filled the bosom of that voluptuous monarch.

The chateau of Chernanceau is built upon arches across the river Cher, whose waters are made to supply the deep moat at each extremity. There is a spacious court-yard in front, from which a draw-bridge conducts to the outer hall of the chateau. There the armor of Francis the First still hangs upon the wall: — his shield, and helm and lance as if the chivalrous but dissolute prince had just exchanged them for the silken robes of the drawing-room. From this hall a door opens into a long gallery, extending the whole length of the building across the Cher. The walls of the gallery are hung with the faded portraits of the long line of the descendants of Hugh Capet; and the windows looking up and down the stream, command a fine reach of pleasant river scenery. This is said to be the only chateau in France, in which the ancient furniture of its original age is preserved. In one part of the building, you are shown the bed-chamber of Diane de Poitiers, with its antique chairs covered with faded damask and embroidery, her bed, and a portrait of the royal favorite hanging over the mantelpiece. In another, you see the apartment of the infamous Catherine de Medici; — a venerable arm-chair, and an autograph letter of Henry the Fourth; — and in an old laboratory, among broken crucibles, and neckless retorts, and drums and trumpets, and skins of wild beasts, and other ancient lumber of various kinds, are to be seen the bed-posts of Francis the First! — Doubtless the naked walls and the vast, solitary chambers of an old and desolate chateau inspire a feeling of greater solemnity and awe; but when the antique furniture of the olden time remains — the faded tapestry on the walls — and the arm-chair by the fire-side, the effect upon the mind is more magical and delightful. The old inhabitants of the place, long gathered to their fathers, though living still in history, seem to have left their halls for the chace or the tournament; and as the heavy door swings upon its reluctant hinge, one almost expects to see the gallant princes and courtly dames enter those halls again, and sweep in stately procession along the silent corridors.

Wrapt in such fancies as these, and gazing on the beauties of this noble chateau, and the soft scenery around it, I lingered unwilling to depart, till the rays of the setting sun, streaming through the dusty windows, admonished me that the day was drawing rapidly to a close. I sallied forth from the southern gate of the chateau — and crossing the broken drawbridge, pursued a pathway along the bank of the river, still gazing back upon those towering walls, now bathed in the rich glow of sunset, till a turn in the road, and a clump of woodland at length shut them out from my sight.

A short time after candle-lighting I reached the little tavern of the Boule d'Or, a few leagues from Tours, where I passed the night. The following morning was lowering and sad. A veil of mist hung over the landscape, and ever and anon a heavy shower burst from the over-burdened clouds, that were driving by before a high and piercing wind. This unpropitious state of the weather detained me until noon; when a cabriolet for Tours drove up, and taking a seat within it, I left the hostess of the Boule d'Or in the middle of a long story about a rich countess, who always alighted there when she passed that way. We drove leisurely along through a beautiful country, till at length we came to the brow of a steep hill, which commands a fine view of the city of Tours and its delightful environs. But the scene was shrouded by the heavy, drifting mist, through which, I could trace but indistinctly the graceful sweep of the Loire, and the spires and roofs of the city far below me.

The city of Tours and the delicious plain in which it lies, have been too often described by other travellers, to render a new description from so listless a pen as mine, either necessary or desirable. After a sojourn of two cloudy and melancholy days, I set out on my return to Paris, by the way of Vendôme and Chartres. I stopped a few hours at the former place, to examine the ruins of a chateau, built by Jeanne d'Albret, mother of Henry the Fourth. It stands upon the summit of a high and precipitous hill, and almost overhangs the town beneath. The French Revolution has completed the ruin, that time had already begun; and nothing now remains but a broken and crumbling bastion, and here and there a solitary tower dropping slowly to decay. In one of these is the grave of Jeanne d'Albret. A marble entablature in the wall above contains the inscription, which is nearly effaced, though enough still remains to tell the curious traveller, that there lies buried the mother of the "Bon Henri." To this is added a prayer, that the repose of the dead may be respected; — a prayer, which has been shamefully disregarded.

Here ended my foot-excursion. The object of my journey was accomplished, and delighted with this short ramble through the Valley of the Loire, I took my seat in the Diligence for Paris, and, on the following day, was again swallowed up in the crowds of the metropolis, like a drop in the bosom of the sea.

THE ANCIENT LYRIC POETRY
OF THE NORTH OF FRANCE.

Quant recommence et revient biaux estez,
Que foille et flor resplendit par boschage,
Que li froiz tanz de l'hyver est passez,
Et cil oisel chantent en lor langage,
Lors chanterai
Et envoisiez serai
De cuer verai.

— Jaques de Chison.

THE TROUVÈRES.

Quant voi la glaie meure,
Et le rosier espanir,
Et sur la bele verdure
La rousée resplendir,
Lors soupir
Pour cele que tant désir.

— Raoul de Soissons.

The literature of France is peculiarly rich in poetry of the olden time. We can trace up the stream of song until it is lost in the deepening shadows of the Middle Ages. Even there it is not a shallow, tinkling rill; but it comes like a mountain stream, rushing and sounding onward through the enchanted regions of romance, and mingles its voice with the tramp of steeds and the brazen sound of arms.

The glorious reign of Charlemagne[3] at the close of the eighth and the commencement of the ninth century, seems to have breathed a spirit of literature as well as of chivalry throughout all France. The monarch established schools and academies in different parts of his realm; and took delight in the society and conversation of learned men. It is amusing to see with what evident

---

3   The following amusing description of this Restorer of Letters, as his biographers call him, is taken from the fabulous Chronicle of John Turpin, chap. xx.

"The Emperor was of a ruddy complexion, with brown hair; of a well-made handsome form, but a stern visage. His height was about eight of his own feet, which were very long. He was of a strong robust make; his legs and thighs very stout, and his sinews firm. His face was thirteen inches long; his beard a palm; his nose half a palm; his forehead a foot over. His lion-like eyes flashed fire like carbuncles; his eye-brows were half a palm over. When he was angry, it was a terror to look upon him. He required eight spans for his girdle, besides what hung loose. He ate sparingly of bread; but a whole quarter of lamb, two fowls, a goose, or a large portion of pork; a peacock, crane, or a whole hare. He drank moderately of wine and water. He was so strong, that he could at a single blow cleave asunder an armed soldier on horseback from the head to the waist, and the horse likewise. He easily vaulted over four horses harnessed together; and could raise an armed man from the ground to his head, as he stood erect upon his hand."

self-satisfaction some of the magi, whom he gathered around him, speak of their exertions in widening the sphere of human knowledge, and pouring in light upon the darkness of their age. "For some," says Alcuin, the director of the school of St Martin de Tours, "I cause the honey of the holy scriptures to flow; I intoxicate others with the old wine of ancient history; these I nourish with the fruits of grammar, gathered by my own hands; and those I enlighten by pointing out to them the stars, like lamps attached by the vaulted ceiling of a great palace!"

Beside this classic erudition of the schools, the age had also its popular literature. Those who were untaught in scholastic wisdom, were learned in traditionary lore; for they had their ballads, in which were described the valor and achievements of the early kings of the Franks. These ballads, of which a collection was made by order of Charlemagne, animated the rude soldier as he rushed to battle, and were sung in the midnight bivouacs of the camp. "Perhaps it is not too much to say" observes the literary historian Schlegel, "that we have still in our possession, if not the original language and form, at least the substance of many of those ancient poems, which were collected by the orders of that prince; — I refer to the Nibelungen Lied, and the collection which goes by the name of the Heldenbuch."

When at length the old Tudesque language, which was the court language of Charlemagne, had given place to the Langue d'Oil, the Northern dialect of the French romance, these ancient ballads passed from the memories of the descendants of the Franks, and were succeeded by the romances of Charlemagne and his Twelve Peers, — of Roland, and Oliver, and the other Paladins, who died at Roncesvalles. Robert Wace, a Norman Trouvère of the twelfth century, says in one of his poems, that a minstrel named Taillefer, mounted on a swift horse, went in front of the Norman army at the battle of Hastings, singing these ancient poems.

These *chansons de geste*, or old historic romances of France, are epic in their character, though without doubt they were written to be chaunted to the sound of an instrument. To what period many of them belong in their present form has never yet been fully determined; and should it finally be proved by phylological research, that they can claim no higher antiquity than the twelfth or thirteenth century, still there can be little doubt that in their original form many of them reached far back into the ninth or tenth. The long prevalent theory, that the romances of the Twelve Peers of France all originated in the fabulous chronicle of Charlemagne and Roland, written by the Archbishop Turpin in the twelfth century, if not as yet generally exploded, is nevertheless fast losing ground.

To the twelfth and thirteenth centuries, also, belong most of the Fabliaux, or metrical tales of the Trouvères. Many of these compositions are remarkable for the inventive talent they display; but as poems they have, generally speaking, little merit, and at times exhibit such a want of refinement, such open and gross obscenity as to be highly offensive.

It is a remarkable circumstance in the literary history of France, that whilst her anti-quarians and scholars have devoted themselves to collecting and illustrating the poetry of the Troubadours, the early lyric poets of the South, that of the Trouvères, or Troubadours of the North, has been almost entirely neglected. By a singular fatality, too, what little time and attention have hitherto been bestowed upon the fathers of French poetry, have been so directed as to save from oblivion little of the most valuable portions of their writings, whilst the more tedious and worthless parts have been brought forth to the public eye, as if to deaden curiosity and put an end to farther research. The ancient historic romances of the land have, for the most part, been left to slumber on unnoticed; whilst the obscene and tiresome Fabliaux have been ushered in to the world as fair specimens of the ancient poetry of France. This has created unjust prejudices in the minds of many against the literature of the olden time, and has led them to regard it as nothing more than a confused mass of coarse and vulgar fictions, adapted to a rude and inelegant state of society.

Of late, however, a more discerning judgment has been brought to the difficult task of ancient research; and in consequence of this the long established prejudices against the crumbling monuments of the national literature of France during the Middle Ages is fast disappearing. Several learned men are engaged in rescuing from oblivion the ancient poetic romances of Charlemagne and the Twelve Peers of France, and their labors seem destined to throw new light not only upon the state of literature, but upon the state of society, during the twelfth and thirteenth centuries.

Among the voluminous remains of Troubadour literature, little else has yet been discovered save poems of a lyric character. The lyre of the Troubodour seems to have responded to the impulse of momentary feelings only, — to the touch of local and transitory circumstances. His song was a sudden burst of excited feeling: — it ceased when the passion was subdued, or rather when its first feverish excitement passed away; and as the liveliest feelings are the most transitory, the songs, which embodied them are short, but full of spirit and energy. On the other hand the great mass of the poetry of the Trouvères is of a narrative or epic character. The genius of the North seems always to have delighted in romantic fiction; and whether we attribute the origin of modern romance to the Arabians or to the Scandanavians, — this at least is certain, that there existed marvellous tales in the nothern languages, and from these, in part at least, the Trouvères imbibed the spirit of narrative poetry. There are no traces of lyric compositions among their writings, till about the commencement of the thirteenth century; and it seems probable that the spirit of song-writing was imbibed from the Troubadours of the South.

Unfortunately the neglect which has so long attended the old historic and heroic romances of the North of France has also befallen in some degree its early lyric poetry. Little has yet been done to discover and bring forth its riches; and doubtless many a sweet little ballad and melancholly complaint lies buried in the dust of the thirteenth century. It is not however my object, in this paper to give an historical sketch of this ancient and almost forgotten poetry, but simply to bring forward a few specimens, which shall exhibit its most striking and obvious characteristics.

In these examples it would be in vain to look for high-wrought expression, suited to the prevailing taste of the present day. Their most striking peculiarity, and perhaps their greatest merit, consists in the simple and direct expression of feeling, which they contain. This feeling, too, is one which breathes the langor of that submissive homage, which was paid to beauty in the days of chivalry; and I am aware that in this age of masculine and matter-of-fact thinking, the love-conceits of a more poetic state of society are generally looked upon as extremely trivial and puerile. Nevertheless I shall venture to present one or two of these simple ballads, which by recalling the distant age wherein they were composed, may peradventure please by the power of contrast.

I have just remarked, that one of the greatest beauties of these ancient ditties is naïveté of thought and simplicity of expression. These I shall endeavor to preserve as far as possible in the translation, though I am fully conscious how much the sparkling beauty of an original loses in being filtered through the idioms of a foreign language.

The favorite theme of the ancient lyric poets of the North of France is the wayward passion of love. They all delight to sing les douces dolors et li mal plaisant de fine amor. With such feelings the beauties of the opening Spring are naturally associated. Almost every love ditty of the old poets commences with some such exordium as this; "When the snows of winter have passed away, when the soft and gentle spring returns, and the flower and leaf shoot in the groves, and the little birds warble to their mates in their own sweet language, — then will I sing my lady-love!

Another favourite introduction to these little rhapsodies of romantic passion, is the approach of morning and its sweet-voiced herald, the lark. The minstrel's song to his lady-love frequently commences with an allusion to the hour,

> 'When the rose-bud opes its e'en,
>   And the blue-bells droop and die,
> And upon the leaves so green
>   Sparkling dew-drops lie.'

The following is at once the simplest and prettiest piece of this kind which I have met with among the early lyric poets of the North of France. It is taken from an anonymous poem entitled "The Paradise of Love." A lover having passed the "live-long night in tears, as he was wont," goes forth to beguile his sorrows with the fragrance and beauty of morning. The carol of the vaulting sky-lark salutes his ear, and to this merry musician he makes his complaint.

> He! aloete,
> Joliete!
> Petit t'est de mes maus.
>
> Hark! hark!
> Pretty lark!
> Little heedest thou my pain!
> But if to these longing arms
> Pitying Love would yield the charms
>   Of the fair
>   With smiling air,
> Blithe would beat my heart again.
>   Hark! hark!
>   Pretty lark!
> Little heedest thou my pain!
> Love may force me still to bear
> While he lists, consuming care,
>   But in anguish
>   Though I languish,

Faithful shall my heart remain.

> *Hark! hark!*
> *Pretty lark!*
> *Little heedest thou my pain!*
> *Then cease, Love, to torment me so; —*
> *But rather than all thoughts forego*
> > *Of the fair*
> > *With flaxen hair,*
> *Give me back her frowns again.*
> > *Hark! hark!*
> > *Pretty lark!*
> *Little heedest thou my pain! —*

Beside the "woful ballad made to his mistress' eyebrow," the early lyric poet frequently indulges in more calmly analyzing the philosophy of love, or in questioning the object and destination of a sigh. Occasionally these quaint conceits are prettily expressed, and the little song flutters through the page like a butterfly. The following is an example.

> *Et on vas tu, petit soupir,*
> *Que j'ai oui si doulcement?*
>
> *And whither goest thou gentle sigh,*
> > *Breathed so softly in my ear?*
> > *Say; dost thou bear his fate severe*
> *To Love's poor martyr doomed to die?*
> *Come; tall me quickly, — do not lie,*
> > *What secret message bringest thou here? —*
> *And whither goest thou, gentle sigh,*
> > *Breathed so softly in my ear? —*
> *May heaven conduct thee to thy will,*
> > *And safely speed thee on thy way;*
> > *This only I would humbly pray —*
> *Pierce deep — but, oh! forbear to kill.*
> *And whither goest thou, gentle sigh,*
> > *Breathed so softly in my ear?*

The ancient lyric poets of France are generally spoken of as a class, and their beauties and defects referred to them collectively and not individually. In truth there are few characteristic marks by which any individual author can be singled out and ranked above the rest. The lyric poets of the thirteenth and fourteenth centuries stand upon nearly the same level. But in the fifteenth century there were two, who surpassed all their contemporaries in the beauty and delicacy of their sentiments; and in the sweetness of their diction, and the structure of their verse, stand far in advance of the age in which they lived. These are Charles d'Orléans and Clotilde de Surville.

Charles, Duke of Orleans, the father of Louis the Twelfth, and uncle of Francis the First, was born in 1391. In the general tenor of his life, the peculiar character of his mind, and his talent for poetry, there is a striking resemblance between this noble poet and James the First of Scotland, his contemporary. Both were remarkable for learning and refinement; — both passed a great portion of their lives in sorrow and imprisonment; and both cheered the solitude of their prison walls with the charms of poetry. Charles d' Orléans was taken prisoner at the battle of Agincourt in 1415, and carried into England, where he remained twenty five years in captivity. It was there, that he composed the greater part of his poetry. In 1440 he returned to France, where he died in 1467.

The poems of this writer exhibit a singular delicacy of thought and sweetness of expression. The following little Renouveaux, or songs on the return of Spring, are full of delicacy and beauty.

> Le temps a laissé son manteau
> De vent, de froidure et de pluye.
>
> Now Time throws off his cloak again
>   Of ermin'd frost, and wind and rain,
>   And clothes him in the embroidery
> Of glittering sun and clear blue sky.
> With beast and bird the forest rings,
>   Each in his jargon cries or sings:
>
> And Time throws off his cloak again
>   Of ermin'd frost, and wind and rain.
> River, and fount, and tinkling brook
>   Wear in their dainty livery
>   Drops of silver jewelry;
> In new made suit they merry look;
> And Time throws off his cloak again
>   Of ermin'd frost, and wind and rain.

The second upon the same subject presents a still more agreeable picture of the departure of Winter and the sweet return of Spring.

Bien monstrez, printemps gracieux,
De quel mestier savez servir.

Gentle Spring! — in sunshine clad,
  Well dost thou thy power display!
For Winter maketh the light heart sad,
  And thou, — thou makest the sad heart gay.
He sees thee — and calls to his gloomy train,
The sleet, and the snow, and the wind, and the rain;
And they shrink away — and they flee in fear,
  When thy merry step draws near.
Winter giveth the fields and the trees so old,
  Their beards of icicles and snow; —
And the rain, it raineth so fast and cold,
  We must cower over the embers low;
And snugly housed from the wind and weather,
Mope like birds that are changing feather

But the storm retires, and the sky grows clear;
  When thy merry step draws near.
Winter maketh the sun in the gloomy sky,
  Wrap him round in a mantle of cloud;
But, Heaven be praised, thy step is nigh;
  Thou tearest away the mournful shroud,
And the earth looks bright — and Winter surly
Who has toiled for naught both late and early,
Is banished afar by the new-born year,
  When thy merry step draws near.

The only person of that age who can dispute the laurel with
Charles d' Orléans is Clotilde de Surville. This sweet poetess was
born in the Bas-Vivarais in the year 1405. Her style is singularly
elegant and correct, and the reader who will take the trouble to
decipher her rude provincial orthography, will find her writings
full of quiet beauty. The following sweet lines, which breathe the
very soul of maternal tenderness, are part of a little poem to her
first born.

O cher enfantelet, vray pourtraict de ton pere!
Dors sur le seyn que ta bousche a pressé.

Sweet babe! true portrait of thy father's face,
  Sleep on the bosom that thy lips have prest!

Sleep, little one; and closely, gently place
Thy drowsy eyelid on thy mother's breast.
Upon that tender eye, my little friend,
Soft sleep shall come, that cometh not to me!
I watch to see thee, nourish thee, defend —
Tis sweet to watch for thee — alone for thee.
His arms fall down; sleep sits upon his brow;
His eye is closed; he sleeps — how still and calm!
Wore not his cheek the apple's ruddy glow,
Would you not say he slept on death's cold arm?
Awake, my boy! — I tremble with affright!
Awake, and chase this fatal thought! — unclose
Thine eye but for one moment on the light!
Even at the price of thine give me repose!
Sweet error! — he but slept — I breathe again —
Come gentle dreams, the hour of sleep beguile!
Oh! when shall he for whom I sigh in vain,
Beside me watch to see thy waking smile?

But upon this theme I have written enough,— perhaps too much.

'This may be poetry for ought I know,
Says an old worthy friend of mine, while leaning
Over my shoulder as I write, although
I can't exactly comprehend its meaning.

I have touched upon the subject before me in a brief and desultory manner, and have purposely left my remarks unencumbered by learned reference and far-sought erudition; for these are ornaments which would ill become so trivial a pen as this wherewith I write, though perchance the want of them will render my essay unsatisfactory to the scholar and the critic. But I am emboldened thus to skim with a light wing over this poetic lore of the past, by the reflection that the greater part of my readers belong not to that grave and serious class, who love the deep wisdom, which lies in quoting from a quaint, forgotten tome, and are ready on all occasions to say, "Commend me to the owl."

THE BAPTISM OF FIRE.
A LEAF FROM HISTORY.

It is a maxim among us Christians, that we cannot possibly suffer any real hurt, if we cannot be convicted of doing any real evil. You may kill, indeed, but you cannot hurt us.

— JUSTIN MARTYR.

THE BAPTISM OF FIRE.

The more you mow us down, the thicker we rise; the
Christian blood you spill is like the seed you sow; — it
springs from the earth again and fructifies the more.
— TERTULLIAN.

As day was drawing to a close, and the rays of the setting sun
climbed slowly up the dungeon wall, the prisoner sat and read in a
tome with silver clasps. He was a man in the vigor of his days, with
a pale and noble countenance, that wore less the marks of worldly
care than of high and holy thought. His temples were already
bald; but a thick and curling beard bespoke the strength of man-
hood, and his eye, dark, full, and eloquent, beamed with all the
enthusiasm of a martyr. The book before him was a volume of the
early Christian Fathers. He was reading the Apologetic of the eloquent Tertullian, the oldest and ablest writer of the Latin Church.
At times he paused, and raised his eyes to heaven as if in prayer,
and then read on again in silence. At length a passage seemed to
touch his inmost soul. He read aloud;

"Give us, then, what names you please, from the instruments
of cruelty you torture us by, call us Sarmenticians and Semaxians,
because you fasten us to trunks of trees, and stick us about with
faggots to set us on fire; yet let me tell you, when we are thus begirt
and dressed about with fire, we are then in our most illustrious
apparel. These are our victorious palms and robes of glory; and
mounted on our funeral pile we look upon ourselves in our triumphal chariot. No wonder, then, such passive heroes please not
those they vanquish with such conquering sufferings. And therefore we pass for men of despair, and violently bent upon our own
destruction. However, that which you are pleased to call madness
and despair in us, are the very actions, which under virtue's stan-
dard lift up your sons of fame and glory, and emblazon them to
future ages."

He arose and paced the dungeon to and fro, with folded arms
and a firm step. His thoughts held communion with eternity.

"Father, which art in Heaven!" he exclaimed; "give me
strength to die, like those holy men of old, who scorned to purchase life at the expense of truth. That truth has made me free;
and though condemned on earth, I know that I am absolved in
heaven!"

He again seated himself at his table, and read in that tome
with silver clasps.

This solitary prisoner was Anne Du Bourg, a man, who feared not man. Once a merciful judge in that august tribunal, upon whose voice hung the life and death of those, who were persecuted for conscience' sake, he was now himself an accused, — a convicted heretic, condemned to the baptism of fire, because he would not unrighteously condemn others. He had dared to plead the cause of suffering humanity before that dread tribunal, and in the presence of the king himself to declare, that it was an offence to the majesty of God to shed man's blood in his name. Six weary months, — from June to December, — he had lain a prisoner in that dungeon, from which a death by fire was soon to set him free. Such was the clemency of Henry the Second!

As the prisoner read, his eyes were filled with tears. He still gazed upon the printed page, but it was a blank before his eyes. His thoughts were far away amid the scenes of his childhood, amid the green valleys of Riom, and the Golden Mountains of Auvergne. Some simple word had called up the vision of the past. He was a child again. He was playing with the pebbles of the brook, — he was shouting to the echo of the hills, — he was praying at his mother's knee, with his little hands clasped in hers.

This dream of childhood was broken by the grating of bolts and bars, as the jailor opened his prison door. A moment afterwards, his former colleague De Harley stood at his side.

"Thou here!" exclaimed the prisoner, surprised at the visit. "Thou in the dungeon of an heretic! On what errand hast thou come?"

"On an errand of mercy," replied De Harley. "I come to tell thee —"

"That the hour of my death draws near?"

"That thou mayst still be saved."

"Yes; if I will bear false witness against my God — barter heaven for earth — an eternity for a few brief days of worldly existence. Lost, thou shouldst say, — lost, not saved!"

"No! saved!" cried De Harley with warmth; "saved from a death of shame and an eternity of wo! Renounce this false doctrine — this abominable heresy — and return again to the bosom of the church, which thou dost rend with strife and dissention."

"God judge between thee and me, which has embraced the truth."

"His hand already smites thee."

"It has fallen more heavily upon those who so unjustly persecute me. Where is the king? — he who said, that with his own eyes he would behold me perish at the stake? — he, to whom the undaunted Du Faur cried, like Elijah to Ahab, It is thou, who troublest Israel! Where is the king? — called through a sudden and violent death to the judgment-seat of heaven! — Where is Minard, the persecutor of the just? — Slain by the hand of an assassin! It was not without reason, that I said to him, when standing before my accusers, Tremble! believe the word of one, who is about to appear before God; thou likewise shalt stand there soon, — thou, that sheddest the blood of the children of peace. — He has gone to his account before me."

"And that menace has hastened thine own condemnation. Minard was slain by the Huguenots, and it is whispered, that thou wert privy to his death."

"This at least might have been spared a dying man!" replied the prisoner, much agitated by so unjust and so unexpected an accusation. "As I hope for mercy hereafter, I am innocent of the blood of this man, and of all knowledge of so foul a crime. But tell me, hast thou come here only to embitter my last hours with such an accusation as this? If so, I pray thee, leave me. My moments are precious. I would be alone."

"I came to offer thee life, freedom, and happiness."

"Life — freedom — happiness! At the price thou hast set upon them, I scorn them all! Had the apostles and martyrs of the early Christian church listened to such paltry bribes as these, where were now the faith in which we trust! These holy men of old shall answer for me. Hear what Justin Martyr says in his earnest appeal to Antonine the Pious, in behalf of the Christians, who in his day were unjustly loaded with public odium and oppression."

He opened the volume before him and read.

"I could wish you would take this also into consideration, that what we say is really for your own good; for it is in our power at any time to escape your torments, by denying the faith, when you question us about it; but we scorn to purchase life at the expense of a lie; for our souls are winged with a desire of a life of eternal duration and purity, of an immediate conversation with God the father and maker of all things. We are in haste to be confessing and finishing our faith; being fully persuaded, that we shall arrive at this blessed state, if we approve ourselves to God by our works, and, by our obedience, express our passion for that divine life, which is never interrupted by any clashing evil."

The Catholic and the Huguenot reasoned long and earnestly together; but they reasoned in vain. Each was firm in his belief; and they parted to meet no more on earth.

On the following day Du Bourg was summoned before his

judges to receive his final sentence. He heard it unmoved, and with a prayer to God, that he would pardon those who had condemned him according to their consciences. He then addressed his judges in an oration full of power and eloquence. It closed with these words.

"And now, ye judges, if indeed you hold the sword of God as ministers of his wrath, to take vengeance upon those who do evil, beware, I charge you beware, how you condemn us. Consider well what evil we have done; and before all things, decide whether it be just, that we should listen unto you, rather than unto God. Are you so drunken with the wine-cup of the great sorceress, that you drink poison for nourishment? Are you not those, who make the people sin, by turning them away from the service of God? And if you regard more the opinion of men than that of heaven, in what esteem are you held by other nations and principalities and powers, for the martyrdoms you have caused in obedience to this blood-stained Phalaris? — God grant, thou cruel tyrant, that by thy miserable death, thou may'st put an end to our groans!

Why weep ye? What means this delay? Your hearts are heavy within you. Your consciences are haunted by the judgment of God. And thus it is, that the condemned rejoice in the fires you have kindled, and think they never live better, than in the midst of consuming flames. Torments affright them not, — insults enfeeble them not, — their honor is redeemed by death — he that dies is the conqueror, and the conquered, he that mourns.

No! whatever snares are spread for us, whatever suffering we endure, you cannot separate us from the love of Christ. Strike then — slay — grind us to powder! Those that die in the Lord shall live again; we shall all be raised together. Condemn me as you will — I am a christian; yes, I am a christian, and am ready to die for the glory of our Lord — for the truth of the evangelists.

Quench, then, your fires! Let the wicked abandon his way, and return unto the Lord, and he will have compassion on him. Live — be happy — and meditate on God, ye Judges! As for me, I go rejoicing to my death. What wait ye for? Lead me to the scaffold!"

They bound the prisoner's hands, and leading him forth from the council-chamber, placed him upon the cart, that was to bear him to the Place de Grève. Before and behind marched a guard of five hundred soldiers; for Du Bourg was beloved by the people, and a popular tumult was apprehended. The day was overcast and sad; and ever and anon the sound of the tolling bell mingled its dismal clang with the solemn notes of the funeral march. They soon reached the place of execution, which was already filled with a dense and silent crowd. In the centre stood the gallows with a pile of faggots beneath it, and the hangman, with a burning torch in his hand. But this funeral apparel inspired no terror in the heart of Du Bourg. A look of triumph beamed from his eye, and his countenance shone like that an angel. With his own hands he divested himself of his outer garments, and gazing round upon the breathless and sympathizing crowd, exclaimed;

"My friends; I come not hither as a thief or a murderer; but it is for the gospel's sake!"

A cord was then fastened round his waist, and he was drawn up into the air. At the same moment the burning torch of the executioner was applied to the faggots beneath, and the thick volumes of smoke concealed the martyr from the horror-stricken crowd. One stifled groan arose from all that vast multitude, like the moan of the sea; and all was hushed again, save the crackling of the faggots, and at intervals the funeral knell, that smote the very soul. The quivering flames darted upward and around; and an agonizing cry broke from the murky cloud;

"My God! My God! forsake me not, that I forsake not thee!"

The wind lifted the reddening smoke, like a veil, and the form of the martyr was seen to fall into the fire beneath, that glowed like a furnace seven times heated. In a moment it rose again, its garments all in flame; and again the faint, half-smothered cry of agony was heard;

"My God! my God! forsake me not, that I forsake not thee!"

Once more the quivering body descended into the flames; and once more it was lifted into the air, a blackened, burning cinder. Again, and again this hellish mockery of baptism was repeated; till the martyr with a despairing, suffocating voice exclaimed;

"O God! I cannot die!"

The chief executioner came forward, and either in mercy to the dying man, or through fear of the populace, threw a noose over his neck, and strangled the almost lifeless victim. At the same moment, the cord which held the body was loosened, and it fell into the fire to rise no more. And thus was consummated the martyrdom of the Baptism of Fire.

COQ-À-L'ÂNE.

Voir, c'est avoir. Allons courir!
  Vie errante
  Est chose enivrante;
Voir, c'est avoir. Allons courir!
Car tout voir, c'est tout conquérir.

Ton œil ne peut se détacher,
  Philosophe
  De mince étoffe,
Ton œil ne peut se détacher
Du vieux coq de ton vieux clocher.

— BERANGER.

COQ-À-L'ÂNE.

My brain methinks is like an hour-glass,
Wherein my imaginations run like sands,
Filling up time; but then are turn'd and turn'd
So that I know not what to stay upon,
And less to put in art.

— Ben Jonson.

A rainy and gloomy winter was just drawing to its close, when I left Paris for the South of France. We started at sunrise; and as we passed along the solitary streets of the vast and silent metropolis, drowsily one by one its clanging horologes chimed the hour of six. Beyond the city gates the wide landscape was covered with a silvery net-work of frost; a wreath of vapor overhung the windings of the Seine; and every twig and shrub, with its sheath of crystal, flashed in the level rays of the rising sun. The sharp frosty air seemed to quicken the sluggish blood of the old postillion and his horses, a fresh team stood ready in harness at each stage, and notwithstanding the slippery pavement of the causeway, the long and tedious climbing the hill-side upwards, and the equally long and tedious descent with chained wheels and the drag, — just after night-fall the lumbering vehicle of Vincent Caillard stopped at the gateway of the Three Emperors in the famous city of Orleans.

I cannot pride myself much upon being a good travelling companion, for the rocking of a coach always lulls me into forgetfulness of the present, and no sooner does the hollow monotonous rumbling of the wheels reach my ear, than like my friend Nick Bottom, "I have an exposition of sleep come upon me." It is not, however, the deep, sonorous slumber of a laborer, "stuffed with distressful bread;" but a kind of day-dream, wherein the creations of fancy seem realities, and the real world, which swims dizzily before the half-shut, drowsy eye, becomes mingled with the imaginary world within. This is doubtless a very great failing in a traveller; and I confess with all humility, that at times the line of demarkation between truth and fiction is rendered thereby so indefinite and indistinct, that I cannot always determine with unerring certainty, whether an event really happened to me, or whether I only dreamed it.

On this account I shall not attempt a detailed description of my journey from Paris to Bordeaux. I was travelling like a bird of passage; and five weary days and four weary nights I was on the way. The diligence stopped only to change horses, and for the travellers to take their meals; and by night I slept with my head under my wing in a snug corner of the coach.

Strange as it may appear to some of my readers, this night-travelling is at times far from being disagreeable. Nay, if the country is flat and uninteresting, and you are favored with a moon, it may be very pleasant. As the night advances the conversation around you gradually dies away, and is imperceptibly given up to some garrulous traveller, who finds himself belated in the midst of a long story, and when at length he puts out his feelers in the form of a question, discovers by the silence around him, that the breathless attention of his audience is owing to their being asleep. All is now silent. You let down the window of the carriage, and the fresh night air cools your flushed and burning cheek. The landscape, though in reality dull and uninteresting, seems beautiful as it floats by in the soft moonshine. Every ruined hovel is changed by the magic of night to a trim cottage, every straggling and dilapidated hamlet becomes as beautiful as those we read of in poetry and romance. Over the lowland hangs a silver mist; over the hills peep the twinkling stars. The keen night air is a spur to the postillion and his horses. In the words of the old German ballad;

> 'Halloo! halloo! away they go,
>   Unheeding wet or dry,
> And horse and rider snort and blow,
>   And sparkling pebbles fly.
> And all on which the moon doth shine
>   Behind them flees afar,
> And backward sped, scuds overhead
>   The sky and every star.

Anon you stop at the relay. The drowsy hostler crawls out of the stable yard; a few gruff words and strange oaths pass between him and the postillion, — then there is a coarse joke in *patois*, of which you understand the ribaldry only, and which is followed by a husky laugh, a sound between a hiss and a growl; — and then you are off again in a crack. Occasionally a way-traveller is uncaged, and a new-comer takes the vacant perch at your elbow. Meanwhile your busy fancy speculates upon all these things, and you fall asleep amid its thousand vagaries. Soon you wake again, and snuff the morning air. It was but a moment, and yet the night is gone. The gray of twilight steals into the window and gives a ghastly look to the countenances of the sleeping group around you. One sits bolt upright in a corner, offending none, and stiff and motionless as an Egyptian mummy; another sits equally straight and immovable, but snores like a priest; the head of a third is dangling over his shoulder, and the tassel of his nightcap tickles his neighbor's ear; a fourth has lost his hat, — his wig is awry, and his under lip hangs lolling about like an idiot's. The whole scene is a living caricature of man, presenting human nature in some of the grotesque attitudes she assumes, when that pragmatical school-master, propriety, has fallen asleep in his chair, and the unruly members of his charge are freed from the thraldom of the rod.

On leaving Orleans, instead of following the great western mail-route through Tours, Poitiers, and Angoulême, and thence on to Bordeaux, I struck across the centre provinces of the Indre, the Haute-Vienne, and the Dordogne, passing through the provincial capitals of Châteauroux, Limoges, and Périgueux. South of the Loire the country assumes a more mountainous aspect, and the landscape is broken by long sweeping hills, and fertile valleys. Many a fair scene invites the traveller's foot to pause; and his eye roves with delight over the picturesque landscape of the valley of the Creuse, and the beautiful highland scenery near Périgueux. There are also many objects of art and antiquity, which arrest his attention. Argenton boasts its Roman amphitheatre, and the ruins of an old castle built by king Pepin; at Chalus the tower, beneath which Richard Cœur-de-Lion was slain, is still pointed out to the curious traveller, and Périgueux is full of crumbling monuments of the Middle Ages.

Scenes like these, and the constant chatter of my fellow-travellers, served to enliven the tedium of a long and fatiguing journey. The French are preeminently a talking people; and every new object afforded a topic for light and animated discussion. The affairs of church and State were, however, the themes oftenest touched upon. The Law Project for the suppression of the liberty of the press was then under discussion in the Chamber of Peers, and excited the most lively interest through the whole kingdom. Of course it was a subject not likely to be forgotten in the stage-coach.

"Ah! mon Dieu!" said a brisk little man, with snow-white hair, and a blazing red face, at the same time drawing up his shoulders to a level with his ears, "The ministry are determined to carry their point at all events. They mean to break down the liberty of the press, cost what it will."

"If they succeed," added the person who sat opposite, "we may thank the Jesuits for it. It is all their work. They rule the mind of our imbecile monarch, and it is their miserable policy to keep the people in darkness."

"No doubt of that," rejoined the first speaker, "Why, no longer ago, than yesterday I read in the Figaro, that a printer had been prosecuted for publishing the moral lessons of the Evangelists without the miracles."

"Is it possible!" said I. "And are the people so stupid as thus patiently to offer their shoulders to the pack-saddle?"

"Most certainly not! — We shall have another revolution."

"If history speaks true, you have had revolutions enough, during the last century or two, to satisfy the most mercurial nation on earth. You have hardly been quiet a moment since the day of the Baracades and the memorable war of the *pots-de-chambre* in the times of the Grand Condé."

"You are pleased to speak lightly of our revolutions, Sir," rejoined the politician, growing warm. "You must, however, confess that each successive one has brought us nearer to our object. Old institutions, whose foundations lie deep in the prejudices of a great nation, are not to be toppled down by the springing of a single mine. You must confess, too, that our national character is much improved since the days you speak of. The youth of the present century are not so frivolous as those of the last. They have no longer that unbounded levity and light-heartedness so generally ascribed to them. From this circumstance we have every thing to hope. Our revolutions, likewise, must necessarily change their character, and secure to us more solid advantages than heretofore."

"Luck makes pluck, as the Germans say. You go on bravely; but it gives me pain to see religion and the church so disregarded."

"Superstition and the church, you mean, Sir;" said the gray-headed man. "Why, Sir, the church is nothing now-a-days, but a tumble-down, dilapidated tower, for rooks, and daws, and such silly birds to build their nests in!"

It was now very evident that I had unearthed a radical; and there is no knowing when his harangue would have ended had not his voice been drowned by the noise of the wheels, as we entered the paved street of the city of Limoges.

A breakfast of boiled capon stuffed with truffles, and accompanied by a *pâté de Périgueux*, a dish well known to French gourmands, restored us all to good humor. While we were at breakfast a personage stalked into the room, whose strange appearance arrested my attention, and gave subject for future conversation to our party. He was a tall, thin figure, armed with a long whip, brass spurs, and black whiskers. He wore a bell-crowned varnished hat, a blue frock-coat with standing collar, a red waistcoat, a pair of yellow leather breeches, and boots, that reached to the knees. I at first took him for a postillion, or a private courier; but, upon inquiry, I found that he was only the son of a Notary Public, and that he dressed in this strange fashion — to please his own fancy.

As soon as we were comfortably seated in the diligence, I made some remark on the singular costume of the personage, whom I had just seen at the tavern.

"These things are so common with us," said the politician, "that we hardly notice them."

"What you want in liberty of speech, then, you make up in liberty of dress."

"Yes; in this, at least, we are a free people."

"I had not been long in France, before I discovered, that a man may dress as he pleases, without being stared at. The most opposite styles of dress seem to be in vogue at the same moment. No strange garment, nor desperate hat excites either ridicule or surprise. French fashions are known and imitated all the world over."

"Very true indeed," said a little man in goslin green. "We give fashions to all other nations."

"Fashions!" said the politician with a kind of growl, "Fashions! — Yes, Sir, and some of us are simple enough to boast of it, as if we were a nation of tailors."

Here the little man in goslin green pulled up the horns of his cotton dicky.

"I recollect," said I, "that your Madame de Pompadour in one of her letters says something to this effect; We furnish our enemies with hair-dressers, ribbons and fashions; and they furnish us with laws."

"That is not the only silly thing she said in her life time. Ah! Sir, these Pompadours, and Maintenons, and Montespans were the authors of much woe to France. Their follies and extravagancies exhausted the public treasury, and made the nation poor. They built palaces, and covered themselves with jewels, and ate from golden plate, whilst the people who toiled for them, had hardly a crust to keep their own children from starvation! And yet they preach to us the divine right of Kings!"

My radical had got upon his high horse again; and I know not whither it would have carried him, had not a thin man with a black, seedy coat, who sat at his elbow, at that moment crossed his path, by one of those abrupt and sudden transitions, which leave you aghast at the strange association of ideas in the speaker's mind.

"*Apropos de bottes!*" exclaimed he. "Speaking of boots, and Notaries Public, and such matters, — excuse me for interrupting you, Sir — a little story has just popped into my head which may amuse the company; and as I am not very fond of political discussions, — no offence, Sir, — I will tell it, for the sake of changing the conversation."

Whereupon, without farther preamble or apology, he proceeded to tell his story in as nearly as may be the following words.

You must know, Gentlemen, that there lived some years ago, in the city of Périgueux, an honest Notary Public, the descendant of a very ancient and broken-down family, and the occupant of one of those old, weather-beaten tenements, which remind you of the times of your great-grandfather. He was a man of an unoffending, sheepish disposition; the father of a family, though not the head of it; for in that family "the hen over-crowed the cock," and the neighbors, when they spake of the Notary, shrugged their shoulders, and exclaimed, "Poor fellow! his spurs want sharpening." In fine, you understand me, Gentlemen; he was a hen-pecked man.

Well — finding no peace at home, he sought it elsewhere, as was very natural for him to do; and at length discovered a place of rest, far beyond the cares and clamors of domestic life. This was a little *café estaminet*, a short way out of the city, whither he repaired every evening, to smoke his pipe, drink sugar-water, and play his favorite game of domino. There he met the boon companions he most loved; heard all the floating chit-chat of the day; laughed when he was in merry mood; found consolation when he was sad; and at all times gave vent to his opinions without fear of being snubbed short by a flat contradiction.

Now, the Notary's bosom friend, was a dealer in claret and cognac, who lived about a league from the city, and always passed his evenings at the estaminet. He was a gross corpulent fellow, raised from a full-blooded Gascon breed, and sired by a comic actor of some reputation in his way. He was remarkable for nothing but his good humor, his love of cards, and a strong propensity to test the quality of his own liquors by comparing them with those sold at other places.

As evil communications corrupt good manners, the bad practices of the wine-dealer won insensibly upon the worthy Notary; and before he was aware of it, he found himself weaned from domino and sugar-water, and addicted to piquet and spiced wine. Indeed it not unfrequently happened, that after a long session at the estaminet, the two friends grew so urbane, that they would waste a full half-hour at the door in friendly dispute, which should conduct the other home.

Though this course of life agreed well enough with the sluggish, phlegmatic temperament of the wine-dealer, it soon began to play the very deuce with the more sensitive organization of the Notary, and finally put his nervous system completely out of tune. He lost his appetite, became gaunt and haggard, and could get no sleep. Legions of blue-devils haunted him by day, and by night strange faces peeped through his bed curtains, and the night-mare snorted in his ear. The worse he grew, the more he smoked and tippled; and the more he smoked and tippled — why, as a matter of course, the worse he grew. His wife alternately stormed — remonstrated — entreated; but all in vain. She made the house too hot for him — he retreated to the tavern; she broke his long-stemmed pipes upon the andirons — he substituted a short-stemmed one, which, for safe keeping, he carried in his waistcoat pocket.

Thus the unhappy Notary ran gradually down at the heel. What with his bad habits and his domestic grievances, he became completely hipped. He imagined that he was going to die; and suffered in quick succession all the diseases, that ever beset mortal man. Every shooting pain was an alarming symptom; — every uneasy feeling after dinner, a sure prognostic of some mortal disease. In vain did his friends endeavor to reason, and then to laugh him out of his strange whims; for when did ever jest or reason cure a sick imagination? His only answer was, "Do let me alone, I know better than you, what ails me."

Well, Gentlemen; things were in this state, when one afternoon in December, as he sat moping in his office, wrapped in an over-coat, with a cap on his head, and his feet thrust into a pair of furred slippers, a cabriolet stopped at the door, and a loud knocking without aroused him from his gloomy revery. It was a message from his friend the wine-dealer, who had been suddenly attacked, the night before, with a violent fever, and growing worse and worse, had now sent in the greatest haste for the Notary to draw up his last will and testament. The case was urgent, and admitted neither excuse nor delay; and the

Notary, tying a handkerchief round his face, and buttoning up to the chin, jumped into the cabriolet, and suffered himself, thought not without some dismal presentiments and misgivings of heart, to be driven to the wine-dealer's house.

When he arrived, he found every thing in the greatest confusion. On entering the house, he ran against the apothecary, who was coming down stairs, with a face as long as your arm, and a pharmaceutical instrument somewhat longer; and a few steps farther, he met the housekeeper — for the wine-dealer was an old bachelor — running up and down, and wringing her hands, for fear that the good man should die — without making his will. He soon reached the chamber of his sick friend, and found him tossing about under a huge pile of bed-clothes, in a paroxysm of fever, calling aloud for a draught of cold water. The Notary shook his head; he thought this a fatal symptom; for ten years back, the wine-dealer had been suffering under a species of hydrophobia, which seemed suddenly to have left him.

When the sick-man saw who stood by his bed-side, he stretched out his hand and exclaimed;

"Ah! my dear friend! have you come at last? — You see it is all over with me. You have arrived just in time to draw up that — that passport of mine. Ah, *grand diable*! how hot it is here! Water — water — water! Will nobody give me a drop of cold water?"

As the case was an urgent one, the Notary made no delay in getting his papers in readiness; and in a short time the last will and testament of the wine-dealer was drawn up in due form, the Notary guiding the sick-man's hand as he scrawled his signature at the bottom.

As the evening wore away, the wine-dealer grew worse and worse, and at length became delirious, mingling in his incoherent ravings the phrases of the Credo and Pater-noster with the shibboleth of the dram-shop and the cardtable.

"Take care! take care! There now — *Credo* in — pop! ting-a-ling-ling! give me some of that. Cent-é-dize! Why you old publican, this wine is poisoned — I know your tricks! — *Sanctam ecclesiam catholicam*. Well, well, we shall see. Imbecil! To have a tiercemajor and a seven of hearts, and discard the seven. By St. Anthony, capot! You are lurched — Ha! ha! I told you so. I knew very well — there — there — don't interrupt me — *Carnis resurrectionem et vitam eternam*!"

With these words upon his lips, the poor wine-dealer expired. Meanwhile the Notary sat cowering over the fire, aghast at the fearful scene, that was passing before him, and now and then striving to keep up his courage by a glass of cognac. Already his fears were on the alert; and the idea of contagion flitted to and fro through his mind. In order to quiet these thoughts of evil import, he lighted his pipe, and began to prepare for returning home. At that moment the apothecary turned round to him, and said;

"Dreadful sickly time, this! The disorder seems to be spreading."

"What disorder!" exclaimed the Notary, with a movement of surprise.

"Two died yesterday, and three to day;" continued the apothecary without answering the question. "Very sickly time, Sir, — very."

"But what disorder is it? What disease has carried off my friend here so suddenly?"

"What disease? Why scarlet fever, to be sure."

"And is it contagious?"

"Certainly!"

"Then I am a dead man!" exclaimed the Notary, putting his pipe into his waistcoat pocket, and beginning to walk up and down the room in despair. "I am a dead man! — Now don't deceive me — don't, will you! — What — what are the symptoms?"

"A sharp, burning pain in the right side," said the apothecary.

"Oh, what a fool I was to come here! Take me home — take me home, and let me die in the bosom of my family!"

In vain did the housekeeper and the apothecary strive to pacify him; — he was not a man to be reasoned with; he answered, that he knew his own constitution better than they did, and insisted upon going home without delay. Unfortunately, the vehicle he came in had returned to the city; and the whole neighborhood was a-bed and asleep. What was to be done? Nothing in the world but to take the apothocary's horse, which stood hitched at the door, patiently waiting his master's will.

Well, Gentlemen; as there was no remedy, our Notary mounted this raw-boned steed, and set forth upon his homeward journey. The night was cold and gusty, and the wind set right in his teeth. Overhead the leaden clouds were beating to and fro, and through them the newly-risen moon seemed to be tossing and drifting along like a cock-boat in the surf; now swallowed up in a huge billow of cloud, and now lifted upon its bosom, and dashed with silvery spray. The trees by the road-side groaned with a sound of evil omen, and before him lay three mortal miles, beset with a thousand imaginary perils. Obedient to the whip and spur, the steed leaped forward by fits and starts, now dashing away in a tremendous gallop, and now relaxing into a long hard trot; while the rider, filled with symptoms of disease, and dire presentiments of death, urged him on, as if he were fleeing before the pestilence.

In this way, by dint of whistling and shouting, and beating right and left, one mile of the fatal three was safely passed. The apprehensions of the Notary had so far subsided, that he even suffered the poor horse to walk up hill; but these apprehensions were suddenly revived again with tenfold violence by a sharp pain in the right side, which seemed to pierce him like a needle.

"It is upon me at last!" groaned the fearstricken man. "Heaven be merciful to me, the greatest of sinners! And must I die in a ditch after all? — He! Get up — get up!"

And away went horse and rider at full speed — hurry-skurry — up hill and down — panting and blowing like all possessed. At every leap, the pain in the rider's side seemed to increase. At first it was a little point like the prick of a needle — then it spread to the size of a half-franc piece — then covered a place as large as the palm of your hand. It gained upon him fast. The poor man groaned aloud in agony; faster and faster sped the horse over the frozen ground — farther and farther spread the pain over his side. To complete the dismal picture, the storm commenced, — snow mingled with rain. But snow, and rain, and cold were naught to him; for though his arms and legs were frozen to icicles, he felt it not; the fatal symptom was upon him; he was doomed to die, — not of cold, but of scarlet fever!

At length, he knew not how, more dead than alive, he reached the gate of the city. A band of ill-bred dogs, that were serenading at a corner of the street, seeing the Notary dash by, joined in the hue and cry, and ran barking and yelping at his heels. It was now late at night, and only here and there a solitary lamp twinkled from an upper story. But on went the Notary, down this street and up that, till at last he reached his own door. There was a light in his wife's bed-chamber. The good woman came to the window, alarmed at such a knocking, and howling, and clattering at her door so late at night; and the Notary was too deeply absorbed in his own sorrows to observe that the lamp cast the shadow of two heads on the window-curtain.

"Let me in! let me in! Quick! quick!" he exclaimed almost breathless from terror and fatigue.

"Who are you, that come to disturb a lone woman at this hour of the night?" cried a sharp voice from above. "Begone about your business, and let quiet people sleep."

"Oh, diable, diable! Come down and let me in! I am your husband. Don't you know my voice? Quick, I beseech you; for I am dying here in the street!"

After a few moments of delay and a few more words of parley, the door was opened, and the Notary stalked into his domicil pale and haggard in aspect, and as stiff and straight as a ghost. Cased from head to heel in an armor of ice, as the glare of the lamp fell upon him, he looked like a knight-errant mailed in steel. But in one place his armor was broken. On his right side was a circular spot, as large as the crown of your hat, and about as black!

"My dear wife!" he exclaimed with more tenderness, than he had exhibited for many years; "Reach me a chair. My hours are numbered. I am a dead man!"

Alarmed at these exclamations, his wife stripped off his over-coat. Something fell from beneath it, and was dashed to pieces on the hearth. It was the Notary's pipe! He placed his hand upon his side, and lo! it was bare to the skin! — Coat, waistcoat and linen were burnt through and through, and there was a blister on his side as large over as your head!

The mystery was soon explained, symptom and all. The Notary had put his pipe into his pocket without knocking out the ashes! And so my story ends.

"Is that all?" asked the radical, when the story-teller had finished.

"That is all."

"Well, what does your story go to prove? What bearing has it on the great interests of man?"

"That is more than I can tell. All I know is that the story is true."

"And did he die?" said the nice little man in goslin green.

"Yes; he died afterwards," replied the story-teller, rather annoyed by the question.

"And what did he die of?" continued goslin-green, following him up.

"What did he die of?" winking to the rest of the company; "Why, he died — of a sudden!"

THE JOURNEY INTO SPAIN.

A l'issue de l'yver que le joly temps de primavère commence, et qu'on voit arbres verdoyer, flems espanouir, et qu' on oit les oisillons chanter en toute joie et deulceur, tant que les verts bocages retentissent de leurs sons et que cœmrs tristes pensifs y dolens s'en esjouissent, s'émeuvent à delaisser deuil et toute tristesse, et se parforcent à valoir mieux.

— *La Plaisante Histoire de Gudrin de Monglave.*

THE JOURNEY INTO SPAIN.

The bud is in the bough,
And the leaf is in the bud,
And Earth's beginning now
In her veins to feel the blood,
Which, warmed by summer's sun
In the alembic of the vine,
From her founts will overrun,
In a ruddy gush of wine.
— Felicia Hemans.

Soft-breathing Spring! how many pleasant thoughts, how many delightful recollections does thy name awaken in the mind of a traveller! Whether he has followed thee by the banks of the Loire or the Guadalquivir, or traced thy footsteps, slowly climbing the sunny slope of Alp or Appenine, the thought of thee shall summon up sweet visions of the past, and thy golden sunshine, and soft, vapory atmosphere become a portion of his day dreams and of him. Sweet images of thee, and scenes that have oft inspired the poet's song, shall mingle in his recollections of the past. The shooting of the tender leaf, — the sweetness and elasticity of the air, — the blue sky and the fleet-drifting cloud, and the flocks of wild fowl, wheeling in long phalanx through the air, and screaming from their dizzy height, — all these shall pass like a dream before his imagination,

'And gently o'er his memory come at times
A glimpse of joys, that had their birth in thee,
Like a brief strain of some forgotten tune.'

It was at the opening of this delightful season of the year, that I passed through the South of France, and took the road of Saint Jean de Luz for the Spanish frontier. I left Bordeaux amid all the noise and gaiety of the last scene of Carnival. The streets and public walks of the city were full of merry groups in masks, — at every corner, crowds were listening to the discordant music of the wandering ballad-singer, and grotesque figures mounted on high stilts and dressed in the garb of the peasants of the Landes of Gascony, were stalking up and down like so many longlegged cranes; — others were amusing themselves with the tricks and grimaces of little monkeys, disguised like little men, bowing to the ladies, and figuring away in red coats and ruffles; — and here and there a band of chimney-sweeps were staring in stupid wonder at the miracles of a showman's box. In a word, all was so full of mirth and merrimake, that even beggary seemed to have forgotten, that it was wretched, and gloried in the ragged masquerade of one poor holiday.

To this scene of noise and gaiety succeeded the silence and solitude of the Landes of Gascony. The road from Bordeaux to Bayonne winds along through immense pine forests, and sandy plains, spotted here and there with a dingy little hovel, and the silence is interrupted only by the dismal, hollow roar of the wind among the melancholy and majestic pines. Occasionally, however, the way is enlivened by a market town or a straggling village; and I still recollect the feelings of delight, which I experienced, when just after sunset we passed through the romantic town of Roquefort, built upon the sides of the green valley of the Douze, which has scooped out a verdant hollow for it to nestle in, amid the barren tracts of sand around.

On leaving Bayonne the scene assumes a character of greater beauty and sublimity. To the vast forests of the Landes of Gascony, succeeds a scene of picturesque beauty, delightful to the traveller's eye. Before him rise the snowy Pyrenees, — a long line of undulating hills,

> *'Bounded afar by peak aspiring bold,*
> *Like giant capt with helm of burnished gold.'*

To the left, as far as the eye can reach, stretch the delicious valleys of the Nive and Adour, and to the right the sea flashes along the pebbly margin of its silver beach, forming a thousand little bays and inlets, or comes tumbling in among the cliffs of a rockbound coast, and beats against its massive barriers, with a distant, hollow, continual roar.

Should these pages meet the eye of any solitary traveller, who is journeying into Spain, by the road I here speak of, I would advise him to travel from Bayonne to Saint Jean de Luz on horse back. At the gate of Bayonne he will find a steed ready caparisoned for him, with a dark eyed Basque girl for his companion and guide, who is to sit beside him upon the same horse. This style of travelling is, I believe, peculiar to the Basque provinces; at all events I have seen it nowhere else. The saddle is constructed with a large frame-work extending on each side, and covered with cushions; and the traveller and his guide being placed on the opposite extremities, serve as a balance to each other. We overtook many travellers mounted in this way, and I could not help thinking it a mode of travelling far preferable to being cooped up in a diligence. The Basque girls are generally beautiful; and there was one of these merry guides, we met upon the road to Bidart, whose image haunts me still. She had large and expressive black eyes, — teeth like pearls, — a rich and sun-burnt complexion, and hair of a glossy blackness, parted on the forehead, and falling down behind in a large braid, so long as almost to touch the ground with the little ribbon, that confined it at the end. She wore the common dress of the peasantry of the South of France, and a large gipsey straw hat was thrown back over her shoulder, and confined by a ribbon about her neck. There was hardly a dusty traveller in the coach, who did not envy her companion, the seat he occupied beside her.

Just at night-fall we entered the town of Saint Jean de Luz, and dashed down its narrow streets at full gallop. The little mad-cap postillion, cracked his knotted whip incessantly, and the sound echoed back from the high, dingy walls like the report of a pistol. The coach-wheels nearly touched the houses on each side of us; — the idlers in the street jumped right and left to save themselves; window-shutters flew open in all directions; a thousand heads popped out from cellar and upper story; *Sacr-r-ré mâtin!* shouted the postillion, — and we rattled on like an earthquake.

Saint Jean de Luz is a smoky little fishing town, situated on the low grounds at the mouth of the Nivelle, and a bridge connects it with the faubourg of Sibourne, which stands on the opposite bank of the river. I had no time, however, to note the peculiarities of the place, for I was whirled out of it, with the same speed and confusion with which I had been whirled in, and I can only recollect the sweep of the road across the Nivelle — the church of Sibourne by the water's edge — the narrow streets — the smoky looking houses, with red window-shutters, and "a very ancient and fish-like smell."

I passed by moonlight the little river Bidasoa, which forms the boundary between France and Spain; and when the morning broke found myself far up among the mountains of San Salvador, the most westerly links of the great Pyrenean chain. The mountains around me were neither rugged nor precipitous; but they rose one above another in a long majestic swell, and the trace of the plough-share was occasionally visible to their summits. They seemed entirely destitute of forest scenery; and as the season of vegetation had not yet commenced, their huge outlines lay black and barren, and desolate against the sky. But it was a glorious morning; and the sun rose up into a cloudless heaven, and poured a flood of gorgeous splendor over the mountain landscape, as if proud of the realm he shone upon. The scene was enlivened by the dashing of a swollen mountain-brook, whose course we followed for miles down the valley, as it leaped onward to its journey's end, now breaking into a white cascade, and now foaming and chafing beneath a rustic bridge. Now and then we rode through a dilapidated town, with a group of idlers at every corner, wrapped in tattered brown cloaks, and smoking their little paper cigars in the sun. Then would succeed a desolate tract of country cheered only by the tinkle of a mule-bell, or the song of a muleteer. Then we would meet a solitary traveller, mounted on horseback, and wrapped in the ample folds of his cloak, with a gun hanging at the pommel of his saddle. Occasionally, too, among the bleak, inhospitable hills, we passed a rude little chapel, with a cluster of ruined cottages around it; and whenever our carriage stopped at the relay, or loitered slowly up the hill-side, a crowd of children would gather around us, with little images and crucifixes for sale, curiously ornamented with ribbons, and little bits of tawdry finery.

A day's journey from the frontier brought us to Vitoria, where the diligence stopped for the night. I spent the scanty remnant of daylight in rambling about the streets of the city, with no other guide but the whim of the moment. Now I plunged down a dark and narrow alley, — now emerged into a wide street, or a spacious market-place, and now aroused the drowsy echoes of a church or cloister with the sound of my intruding footsteps. But descriptions of churches and public squares are dull and tedious matters for those readers, who are in search of amusement and not of instruction; and if any one has accompanied me thus far on my fatiguing journey towards the Spanish capital, I will readily excuse him from the toil of an evening ramble through the streets of Vitoria.

On the following morning we left Vitoria long before daybreak, and during our forenoon's journey, the postillion drew up at a relay, on the southern slope of the Sierra de San Lorenzo in the province of Old Castile. The house was an old, dilapidated tenement, built of rough stone, and coarsely plastered upon the outside. The tiled roof had long been the sport of wind and rain, the motley coat of plaster was broken and time-worn, and the whole building sadly out of repair; though the fanciful mouldings under the eaves, and the curiously carved wood-work, that supported the little balcony over the principal entrance, spoke of better days gone by. The whole building reminded me of a dilapidated Spanish Don, down at the heel and out at elbows, but with here and there a remnant of former magnificence peeping through the loopholes of his tattered cloak.

A wide gate-way ushered the traveller into the interior of the building, and conducted him to a low-roofed apartment, paved with round stones, and serving both as a court-yard and a stable. It seemed to be a neutral ground for man and beast; — a little republic, where horse and rider had common privileges, and mule and muleteer lay cheek by jowl. In one corner a poor jackass was patiently devouring a bundle of musty straw, — in another its master lay sound asleep with his saddle-cloth for a pillow; here, a group of muleteers were quarrelling over a pack of dirty cards, — and there the village barber with a self-important air, stood laving the alcalde's chin from the helmet of Mambrino. On the wall a little taper glimmered feebly before an image of Saint Anthony; directly opposite these, a leathern wine-bottle hung by the neck from a pair of ox-horns; and the pavement below was covered with a curious medley of boxes, and bags, and cloaks, and pack-saddles, and sacks of grain, and skins of wine, and all kinds of lumber.

A small door upon the right led us into the inn-kitchen. It was a room about ten feet square, and literally all chimney; for the hearth was in the centre of the floor, and the walls sloped upward in the form of a long tapering pyramid, with an opening at the top for the escape of the smoke. Quite round this little room ran a row of benches, upon which sat one or two grave personages smoking paper cigars. Upon the hearth blazed a handful of faggots, whose bright flame danced merrily among a motley congregation of pots and kettles, and a long wreath of smoke wound lazily up through the huge tunnel of the roof above. The walls were black with soot, and ornamented with sundry legs of bacon and festoons of sausages; and as there were no windows in this dingy abode, the only light, which cheered the darkness within, came flickering from the fire upon the hearth, and the smoky sunbeams, that peeped down the long-necked chimney.

I had not been long seated by the fire, when the tinkling of mule bells, the clatter of hoofs, and the hoarse voice of a muleteer in the outer apartment announced the arrival of new guests. A few moments afterward, the kitchen door opened and a person entered, whose appearance strongly arrested my attention. It was a tall athletic figure, with the majestic carriage of a grandee, and a dark sun-burnt countenance, that indicated an age of about fifty years. His dress was singular, and such as I had not before seen. He wore a round hat, with wide flapping brim, from beneath which his long black hair hung in curls upon his shoulders; a leather jerkin, with cloth sleeves, descended to his hips; around his waist was closely buckled a leather belt, with a cartouche-box on one side; a pair of Marmeluke pantaloons of black serge hung in ample folds to the knees, around which they were closely gathered by embroidered garters of blue silk; and black broadcloth leggings, buttoned close to the calves, and strapped over a pair of brown leather shoes, completed the singular dress of the stranger. He doffed his hat as he entered, and saluting the company with a *"Dios guarde á Ustedes, caballeros,"* (God guard you, gentlemen) took a seat by the fire, and entered into conversation with those around him.

As my curiosity was not a little excited by the peculiar dress of this person, I inquired of a travelling companion, who sat at my elbow, who and what this new-comer was. From him I learned that he was a muleteer of the Maragatería, a name given to a cluster of small towns which lie in the mountainous country between Astorga and Villafranca, in the western corner of the kingdom of Leon.

"Nearly every province in Spain," said he, "has its peculiar costume, as you will see, when you have advanced farther into our country. For instance, the Catalonians wear crimson caps, hanging down upon the shoulder like a sack; wide pantaloons of green velvet, long enough in the waistband to cover the whole breast; and a little strip of a jacket, made of the same material, and so short as to bring the pocket directly under the arm-pit. The Valencians, on the contrary, go almost naked; a linen shirt, wide linen trowsers, reaching no lower than the knees, and a pair of coarse leather sandals complete their simple garb; it is only in mid-winter, that they indulge in the luxury of jacket. The most beautiful and expensive costume, however, is that of Andalusia. It consists of a velvet jacket, faced with rich, and various-colored embroidery, and covered with tassels and silken cord; a vest of some gay color; a silken handkerchief round the neck, and a crimson sash round the waist; breeches, that button down each side; gaiters and shoes of white leather; and a handkerchief of bright-colored silk wound round the head like a turban, and surmounted by a velvet cap, or a little round hat, with a wide band, and an abundance of silken loops and tassels. The Old Castilians are more grave in their attire. They wear a leather breast-plate instead of a jacket; a montera cap, breeches and leggings. This fellow is a Maragato; and in the villages of the Maragatería the costume varies a little from the rest of Leon and Castile."

"If he is indeed a Maragato," said I jestingly, "who knows, but he may be a descendant of the muleteer, who behaved so naughtily at Cacabelos, as related in the second chapter of the veracious history of Gil Blas de Santillana."

"¿Quien sabe?" was the reply. "Notwithstanding the pride, which even the meanest Castillian feels in counting over a long line of good-for-nothing ancestors, the science of genealogy has become of late a very intricate study in Spain."

Here our conversation was cut short by the mayoral of the diligence, who came to tell us, that the mules were waiting; and before many hours had elapsed, we were scrambling through the square of the ancient city of Burgos. On the morrow we crossed the river Duero and the Guadarama mountains, and early in the afternoon entered the *"Heroica Villa"* of Madrid by the Puerta de Fuencarral.

www.ingramcontent.com/pod-product-compliance
Lightning Source LLC
LaVergne TN
LVHW011207080426
835508LV00007B/657